Rhona Snelling

Edu Breakout Englisch

Escape Games für die 9./10. Klasse

Alles Digitale zu diesem Buch kann auf der Lernplattform **allango** von Ernst Klett Sprachen abgerufen werden. So geht's:

QR-Code scannen oder **www.allango.net** aufrufen

Zur Aktivierung zusätzlicher Komponenten geben Sie bitte folgenden Lizenzschlüssel ein:

EKS-506685-f173-8e3a-3a9b

Weitere Informationen dazu finden Sie unter: **www.allango.net**

Dieses Symbol bedeutet, dass zu einem Buch-Abschnitt ein digitaler Inhalt verfügbar ist.

Ernst Klett Sprachen

Stuttgart

Bildquellenverzeichnis:
7 123RF.com (timhester), Nidderau; **9.1** Getty Images (chameleonseye), München; Cover 123RF.com (fredex8); **9.2** 123RF.com (rumandawi); **9.3** Getty Images (Beverley Van Praagh); **10.1, 39** 123RF.com (annaartistt); **10.2** 123RF.com (sensay); **13** 123RF.com (rtsubin); **15.1** 123RF.com (pikepicture); **15.2** 123RF.com (pikepicture); **15.3** 123RF.com (pikepicture); **15.4** 123RF.com (vitalinagerman); **15.5** 123RF.com (pikepicture); **15.6** 123RF.com (pikepicture); **23.1** 123RF.com (Aleksandr Glushchenko); **23.2** Getty Images (lemur4eg); **23.3** 123RF.com (miceking); **23.4** 123RF.com (grynold); **23.5** 123RF.com (ekaterinabaikal); **23.6** 123RF.com (luisrftc); **24** 123RF.com (hobbitfoot); **25** 123RF.com (devidgrutz); **27, 73** 123RF.com (yupiramos); **28.1** Getty Images (Olesya Chesnokova); **28.2** Getty Images (Magnilion); **28.3** Getty Images (Anya Filipeva); **28.4** Getty Images (Iryna Shancheva); **28.5** Getty Images (Magnilion); **31.1, 69.2** Getty Images (kolotuschenko); **31.2** 123RF.com (vivat191192); **36.1** 123RF.com (viktorijareut); **37** 123RF.com (praewpailin); **40.1, 41.1** 123RF.com (nastyatrel); **40.2, 41.2** 123RF.com (azzardo); **40.3, 41.3** 123RF.com (wirakorn); **43** 123RF.com (floralset); **44.1, 45, 57.1, 79, 80, 81, 83** 123RF.com (jenjawin); **44.2** 123RF.com (saryuuu10); **47** 123RF.com (peshkov); **48** 123RF.com (bplanet); **49** 123RF.com (noche); **51** 123RF.com (solarus); **55** 123RF.com (putracetol); **56** 123RF.com (ssstocker); **57.2** 123RF.com (vectorspman); **57.3** 123RF.com (yayayoy); **57.4** 123RF.com (yayayoy); **57.5** 123RF.com (yayayoy); **57.6** 123RF.com (yayayoy); **57.7** 123RF.com (yayayoy); 63, 64, 65.2 **123RF.com (honksantima)**; 65.1 **123RF.com (simva)**; 65.3 **123RF.com (eugenebsov)**; 69.1 **123RF.com** (jang9159); 71 **123RF.com (armstockers)**; 74.1, 76.1 **Getty Images (photosynthesis)**; 74.2, 76.3 **Getty Images (photosynthesis)**; 74.3, 76.6 Getty Images (Vadym Kalitnyk); 74.4, 76.4 Getty Images (photosynthesis); 74.5, 76.5 Getty Images (photosynthesis); 75, 76.2 123RF.com (bsd555); 77 Getty Images (FallenKnight)

1 Auflage 1 5 4 3 2 1 | 2028 27 26 25 24

Alle Drucke dieser Auflage sind unverändert und können im Unterricht nebeneinander verwendet werden.

Autorin: Rhona Snelling

Redaktion: Wolfgang Volz
Layoutkonzeption: Maja Merz
Gestaltung und Satz: Typoint, Berlin
Umschlaggestaltung: Maja Merz
Titelbild: 123RF.com (fredex8, katisa), Nidderau
Tonregie und Schnitt: Acadecraft, India
Druck und Bindung: Elanders GmbH, Waiblingen

Printed in Germany

ISBN 978-3-12-506685-4

Contents

Introduction

What are "escape games"?

Escape games involve students working together to find solutions to problems, and, ultimately, to 'escape' a specific situation or to 'break out'. Not only are problem-solving, critical thinking and teamwork skills required, but also the ability to understand and use language effectively during the task.

How do escape games improve students' language skills?

Studies show that escape games offer excellent learning opportunities and increased motivation for students; escape games should not be dismissed as 'just' games.

The collaborative nature of escape games means that teamwork is naturally fostered and developed alongside communicative competence and interpersonal skills, such as turn-taking, listening to others, expressing opinions, etc. This also helps to strengthen relationships with others, build confidence and lower anxiety.

As well as integrating reading, writing, speaking and listening skills, each escape game in this book contains a clear and identifiable language focus. Grammatical structures and vocabulary expected at this level are included and practised throughout. The language practice occurs in a natural and contextualised manner and as the simple result of taking part in an immersive escape game.

Why use this book?

All the escape games are:

- **easy to use**
  The photocopiable activities in this book are especially designed for use in the English language classroom. The activities are designed to be easily set up and the instructions are clear and concise.

- **entertaining and engaging**
  The activities are more than just a fun extension to the coursebook. Developing skills and language simultaneously, each activity is based on language that can be expected at this level and explores a range of topics commonly found in the coursebook. Set in a range of contexts, students can learn about English-speaking countries and other cultures.

- **motivating**
  Your students may be too involved in playing the escape game to realise that they are practising the language you have already introduced. They may instead be too focused on working together to solve the puzzles to even notice that they are using the target language.

How to use this book

The twenty escape games in this book can be used in any order, as all the structures are appropriate for students at this level.

Therefore, you may wish to select a particular language point or a specific topic for your students, or you may wish to follow the numerical order of the escape games.

Procedure

Make a copy of the worksheets (for each part of the escape game) for each student in your class.

Put students in small groups. Explain the situation and give each student WS1. Students work together to solve the puzzle on the worksheet in order to get the code and unlock the padlock (at the bottom of each worksheet). If a group is struggling and asks for your help, you can give them the first clue, then the second clue, and, finally, the third clue. (They need to mark the box at the top of the worksheet with how many clues they used before solving the puzzle.)

When they produce the correct code for WS1, you can give them the next worksheet (WS2 or WS2A and WS2B). The groups solve another puzzle (asking you for clues, if necessary) in order to finish the escape game and/or continue to the final worksheet (WS3).

The group who cracks the code and 'escapes' first, using the lowest number of clues, is the winning team.

During the escape game, your role as a teacher is to observe the groups working together and check codes or provide clues, and hand out the next worksheets.

Differentiation

The students in your class may have different levels of language competency as well as different levels of confidence. Less able or less confident students benefit from the focus of the activity being on task completion and collaboration as opposed to linguistic accuracy.

You can give groups who finish early, a related extension task. Some generic tasks include:

- write about their own life using examples of the target language,
- make a simple drawing of an image on the worksheet and describe it,
- record any new language in their notebook,
- devise their own puzzle for another student to solve.

Specific differentiation tasks are also provided with each escape game.

Special Days 1 – Australia Day

Can you solve the puzzle?

Rationale

The students practise their reading and speaking skills to complete these puzzles. They also practise their basic writing skills.

Students practise and revise the passive whilst learning about Australia Day and animals found in Australia.

Situation

In EG1–2, students learn about special days of celebration and tradition in other countries. In Worksheet 1, students are talking online with their friend in Australia and solve a word puzzle about kangaroos. In Worksheet 2, students solve a word puzzle to complete sentences about Australia Day. In Worksheet 3, students complete an information sheet about koala bears.

Differentiation

You can give groups who finish early, a related extension task.

For example:

- Worksheet 1: Students write five passive sentences about a species of animal – the sentences can be factual or imaginary.
- Worksheet 2: Students write five passive sentences about a national day – real or imaginary.
- Worksheet 3: Students choose five sentences from their extension tasks for Worksheet 1 and 2, and rewrite them as word puzzles (in the style of Worksheet 3). Students then swap with a partner and complete the sentences.

Solutions

Worksheet 1

thumb**biten**s**hopping**th**islands**pro**joeys**ga**meat**lantic**plants**un**visitors**

1 islands
2 joeys
3 hopping
4 bite
5 meat
6 plants
7 visitors

Worksheet 2

1 consider
2 present
3 link
4 give
5 choose
6 remember

A remembered
B given
C ***organised***
D chosen
E presented
F linked
G considered

Worksheet 3

1 is used
2 is loved
3 are being made
4 are observed
5 are consumed

Language focus

- passive voice

Codes & clues

WS 1 4 1 1
Clue 1
Each word in the puzzle has some letters before and after that you do not need.

Clue 2
The passive is formed with *to be* + past participle.

Clue 3
The form of the verb *to be* must match the subject.

WS 2 4 2 1
Clue 1
Each verb in the puzzle is in the infinitive form.

Clue 2
The passive is formed with *to be* + past participle form of the verb.

Clue 3
Read the sentences. What is the tense of the missing verb?

WS 3 3 0 1
Clue 1
The passive is formed with *to be* + past participle.

Clue 2
Change the form of *to be* to the correct tense.

Clue 3
The past participles of irregular verbs do not follow the same spelling rules as regular verbs.

Clues used ✓		
①	②	③

Can you solve the puzzle?

Situation

You have a new online friend, Bruce, who lives in Queensland, Australia. Bruce is a **volunteer** at Australia Zoo. He is organising an online tour of the zoo and he needs your help with the tour. He wants to 'test' some of the tour with you.

You are on a video call with Bruce. He is outside the kangaroo **enclosure**. You have to complete the sentences with the seven missing words in the puzzle … and then you can enter the kangaroo enclosure.

volunteer *Freiwillige(r)* • **enclosure** *Gehege*

Can you complete the sentences with the seven missing words in the puzzle?

thumbitenshoppingthislandsportjoeysgameatlanticplantsunvisitorso

1 Kangaroos are found in Australia and some nearby ____________.

2 ____________ (baby kangaroos) will be carried by their mothers until they are about 10 months old.

3 Their ____________ motion is created by their powerful hind legs and their long tail.

4 Kangaroos have been known to kick, punch or ____________ to defend themselves.

5 Kangaroo ____________ is eaten in some countries.

6 Kangaroos are herbivores and eat grass and ____________.

7 Kangaroos can be fed by ____________ to the zoo.

What is the missing code? Write the letters and unlock the padlock!

- the number of sentences with the present passive
- the number of sentences without the passive
- the number of sentences with the present perfect passive

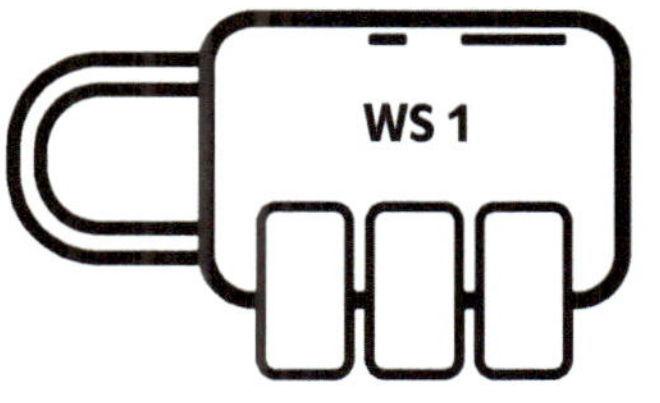

ISBN 978-3-12-506685-4

Clues used ✓		
①	②	③

Can you complete the puzzle?

Situation

Well done! You have completed the sentences and you are now in the kangaroo enclosure!

Bruce shows you around the enclosure. There are lots of visitors there today. He explains that it is Australia Day and this is why the zoo is very busy.

Bruce tells you some facts about Australia Day. He gives you a puzzle of missing verbs to complete the facts. If you solve the puzzle and complete the facts, he will take you to another part of the tour – the koala bears' enclosure.

Can you complete the six verbs and facts A–G?

1				C		N	S		D		R
2				P	R			E	N		
					A						
3			L		N	K					
4				G		V					
5	C	H			S						
6		R		M		M			R		

A The anniversary of the arrival of the first British ships in New South Wales (26 January 1788) **is** .... every year.

B It is a public holiday across the country, so many employees **have been** .... the day off. (The zoo is open today – it only closes one day a year and that's Christmas Day!)

C Various cultural events, including concerts, festivals, sports competitions, and fireworks displays **are** .... for Australia Day.

D Australia Day **is** frequently .... for citizenship ceremonies. This ceremony is for new citizens to officially become 'Australian'.

E On Australia Day, the 'Australian of the Year' award **will be** .... The awards are for Australians who have made outstanding contributions to their community.

F Another event that **has been** .... with Australia Day is the 'Hottest 100'. It occurs the day after Australia Day and it is an annual poll of the nation's favourite 100 songs of the past year.

G However, Australia Day **is** .... **to be** a sad and controversial day by some people. For example, some indigenous Australians believe the arrival of the British ships has been very harmful to the Indigenous population.

What is the missing code? Write the numbers of past participles with three syllables, two syllables and one syllable and unlock the padlock!

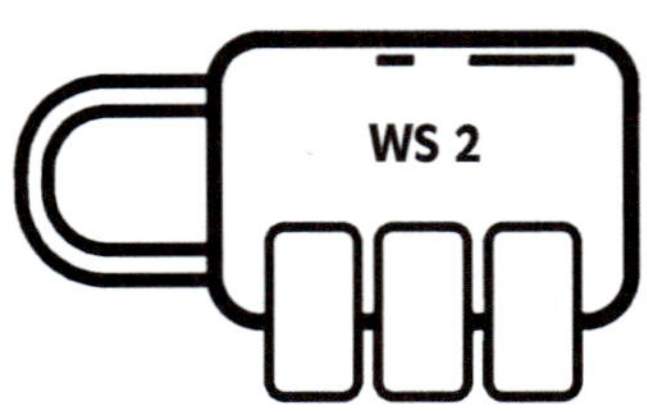

Edu Breakout Englisch – Escape Games für die 9./10. Klasse
ISBN 978-3-12-506685-4

Alles Digitale auf allango.net

Can you complete the facts?

Clues used ✓		
①	②	③

Situation

Well done! You have solved the puzzles and completed the sentences! You are now in the koala bears' enclosure!

Bruce explains these animals are very popular with visitors, because people can hold and **stroke** them. He has written an information sheet about koala bears for the tour. There is another puzzle in the information sheet.

Can you find the verbs in brackets and use the passive form to complete the sentences?

to stroke *streicheln*

Can you complete the sentences with the passive form of the verbs in brackets?

KOALA BEARS – FIVE FUN FACTS

1 The term 'marsupials' .... *(eus)* for koala bears, because they raise and carry their babies in pouches, like kangaroos.

2 The cute appearance of koala bears .... *(evlo)* by everyone!

3 Koala bears are protected by law in Australia. Efforts .... *(aekm)* to protect and conserve their habitats.

4 Koala bears .... occasionally .... *(beeorsv)* in urban areas rather than trees.

5 Eucalyptus leaves are the primary food source of koala bears, and they .... *(cemnosu)* in large quantities by koalas.

What is the missing code? Write the numbers and unlock the padlock!

- the number of *are* in the answers
- the number of *been* in the answers
- the number of *being* in the answers

WS 3

Alles Digitale auf **allango.net**

Edu Breakout Englisch – Escape Games für die 9./10. Klasse
ISBN 978-3-12-506685-4

Special Days 2 – Indigenous People's Day

Can you work out the title?

Rationale

The students practise their reading and writing skills to complete these puzzles.

Students practise and revise cleft sentences beginning with *What* whilst learning about Indigenous People's Day.

Situation

In EG1–2, students learn about special days of celebration and tradition in other countries. In Worksheet 1, students use a note to work out the title of a book. In Worksheet 2, students match words to make sentences about indigenous languages. In Worksheet 3, students complete sentences about Indigenous People's Day.

Differentiation

You can give groups who finish early, a related extension task. For example:

- Worksheet 1: Students write a definition for 'indigenous people' and/or make notes on what they know about indigenous people and what they would like to know about indigenous people.
- Worksheet 2: Students choose three sentence beginnings and complete the sentences with their own ideas.
- Worksheet 3: Students turn their worksheets over and write as many facts as they can about Indigenous Peoples Day

Solutions

Worksheet 1

What we can learn (from indigenous people)

Worksheet 2

1 D
2 A
3 C
4 G
5 B
6 E
F = extra

Worksheet 3

1 What, was
2 What, is
3 What, are
4 What, is
5 What, is
6 What, was

Language focus

- emphasis: cleft sentences beginning with *What*

Codes & clues

WS 1 1 1 4
Clue 1
Each gap (_) represents one word.

Clue 2
You only need one letter from each word.

Clue 3
The first letters of each word make another word.

WS 2 1 2 9
Clue 1
The tense of the sentence beginning must match the tense of the sentence ending.

Clue 2
Use the main verb in the sentence beginning to help you find the sentence ending with the relevant information.

Clue 3
The beginning and ending of the sentence must make sense when they are joined together.

WS 3 3 1 2
Clue 1
Cleft sentences begin with *What*.

Clue 2
The main verb at the beginning of the sentence indicates the correct tense of to be.

Clue 3
Read your completed sentence and make sure the tenses make sense.

Clues used ✓		
①	②	③

Can you work out the title?

Situation

You are in the library at school. You have been doing your homework for a long time. It's late and it's cold. You are tired and hungry. You get up and pack your bag. It's time to go home.

You are walking towards the door when you hear something behind some shelves. You walk behind the shelves and see a very old, **dusty** book on the floor. You pick it up and see that part of the **title** is missing. What an unusual book this is! You open the book and find a small note inside.

dusty *staubig* • **title** *Titel*

Can you use the note to work out the title?

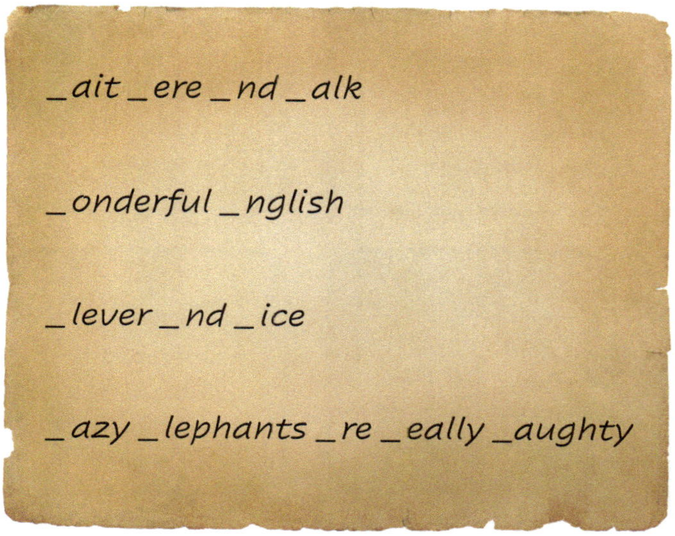

What is the missing code? Write the numbers and unlock the padlock!

- the number of modal verbs in the title
- the number of subject pronouns in the title
- the total number of syllables in the four missing words in the title

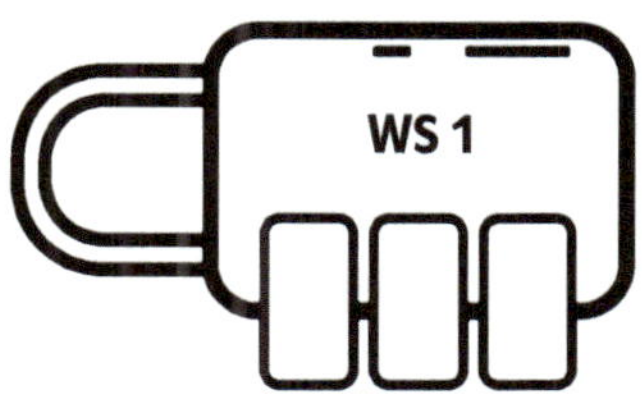

Edu Breakout Englisch – Escape Games für die 9./10. Klasse
ISBN 978-3-12-506685-4

Clues used ✓		
①	②	③

Can you match the sentences?

Situation

Well done! You worked out the title of the book!

You **flick through** the pages of the book and start reading about **indigenous people**. You hear **footsteps**. The librarian is walking over to you and you have a conversation about indigenous people.

The librarian knows you like puzzles, so he gives you two sets of cards about indigenous languages.

flick through *durchblättern* • **indigenous people** *Ureinwohner* • **footstep** *Schritt*

Can you match 1 – 6 and A – G to make sentences? There is one extra ending that you do not need.

1 What makes indigenous people special is …

2 What often surprises people about indigenous languages is …

3 What role language plays in shaping and supporting culture has been …

4 What contributes to the richness of indigenous languages are …

5 What encourages indigenous people to protect their language is …

6 What challenges the dominance of other global languages, like English, is …

A … that there are around 7.000 of them spoken throughout the world.

B … their wish to pass on their native languages to future generations.

C … something various scientists have been exploring for many years.

D … their love for their country and their unique cultural background, including their language.

E … the increasing understanding of the importance of other people and their languages.

F … how to look after the children of indigenous people.

G … their diverse language structures and cultural expressions.

What is the missing code? Write the numbers and unlock the padlock!

- the total number of nouns in the ending for item 2
- the total number of prepositions in the ending for item 6
- the total number of words in the extra ending

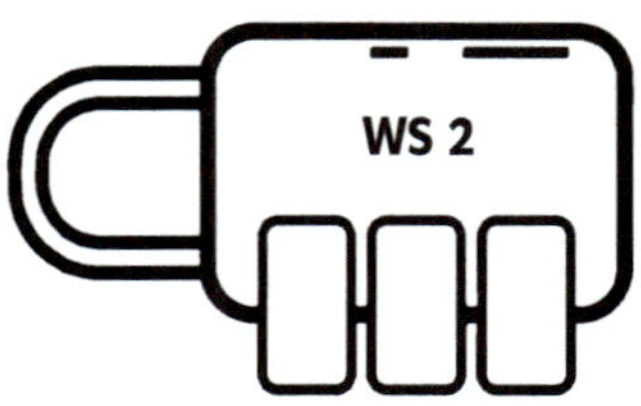

Edu Breakout Englisch – Escape Games für die 9./10. Klasse
ISBN 978-3-12-506685-4

Alles Digitale auf allango.net

Clues used ✓		
①	②	③

Can you complete the information?

Situation

Well done! You matched the sentences!

The librarian shows you another book and asks for your help. Some of the pages are **torn** and some of the words are missing or **smudged**. The librarian would like you to type the sentences, so that he can print the sentences and keep them with the book.

torn *zerrissen* • **smudged** *verschmutzt*

Can you add *What* and the correct form of *to be* to the sentences?

Indigenous Peoples Day

In the USA, *Indigenous Peoples Day* is observed on the second Monday in October. The *International Day of the World's Indigenous Peoples* is observed on 9 August.

1 American President Joe Biden recognised in his speech about Indigenous Peoples Day the historical unfairness experienced by native people after settlers arrived.

2 is celebrated on this day the history and culture of indigenous people.

3 is also discussed the ongoing challenges experienced by native people.

4 happens on this day a variety of cultural performances and educational activities.

5 many American states have done to replace the Columbus Day with Indigenous Peoples Day.

6 used to happen on Columbus Day holding parades in cities to celebrate the arrival of Christopher Columbus to the USA in 1492.

What is the missing code? Write the numbers and unlock the padlock!

- the number of *is* in the answers
- the number of *are* in the answers
- the number of *was* in the answers

WS 3

Edu Breakout Englisch –
Escape Games für die 9./10. Klasse
ISBN 978-3-12-506685-4

Find the influencer

Can you guess the location?

Rationale

The students practise their reading and writing skills to complete these puzzles. They also practise their speaking skills and communication skills in Worksheet 2A and 2B.

Students practise and revise dependent prepositions through the context of a video shoot by social media star Younes Zarou.

Situation

In Worksheet 1, students guess missing words to find the location of Younes Zarou's next shoot. In Worksheet 2A and 2B, students work together to complete and match questions and answers.

Differentiation

You can give groups who finish early, a related extension task. For example:

- Worksheet 1: Students write a response to the comments using one of the dependent prepositions or another dependent preposition.
- Worksheet 2A: Students write the answers for each of the questions.
- Worksheet 2B: Students write the question for each of the answers.

Solutions

Worksheet 1

1 to
2 about
3 park
4 to
5 with
6 of
7 about
8 to
9 for

Worksheet 2A and 2B

1 in / E in
2 in, on / G at, of, in
3 on / A by
4 with, of / F on, to
5 of, about / D about, for
6 with, for / C in, of, in
7 to, to / B about, with

Language focus

- dependent prepositions (after nouns, adjectives and verbs)

Codes & clues

WS 1 2 2 3
Clue 1
The missing words are dependent prepositions. These are specific combinations of a verb, adjective or noun and a preposition

Clue 2
The preposition to appears three times and the preposition *about* appears twice.

Clue 3
The other prepositions begin with the letters *f, o,* and *w*.

WS 2A 8 4 1
Clue 1
You need seven prepositions to complete the questions.

Clue 2
Five prepositions are used twice.

Clue 3
The other two prepositions begin with the letters *a* and *f*.

WS 2B 3 5 7
Clue 1
You need a different preposition to complete each of the answers.

Clue 2
Six of the prepositions have two letters.

Clue 3
The other two prepositions begin with the letters *a* and *w*.

Can you guess the location?

Clues used ✓		
①	②	③

Situation

You are a big fan of TikTok star Younes Zarou. There is a **rumour** that he is making a video near your home. You want to go and watch, but you don't know the location. You see another fan's social media post. Some words, including the location, are hidden.

rumour *Gerücht*

Can you guess the missing words and the location?

ED According (1) ______ his Instagram account, Younes is going to be in our home city this weekend! I'm very excited (2) ______ it! Where's he going to be? Does anyone know?

AMINA It's a secret, but ... he'll be at the (3) _ _ _ _ .
- The first letter is in place, but not in location.
- The second letter is a vowel (and also an indefinite article).
- The third letter is in road and also in route.
- The final letter is in kind, but not in nice.

LEON **@AMINA** 😀 Nice, Amina! I've been talking (4) ______ some other fans and you're right. He'll be there in the early hours of Saturday morning.

HANNAH **@AMINA** I don't want to disagree (5) ______ you, but that's not possible. The gates are locked at midnight.

DANI **@HANNAH** Oh no! I'm afraid (6) ______ the dark! I'm not going! 😀

LEON **@DANI** Don't worry (7) ______ the dark! There's a solution (8) ______ that problem – take a torch!

AMINA **@HANNAH** Well, Younes has a reputation (9) ______ planning his videos carefully. I'm sure he has permission to be there after it's closed.

What is the missing code? Write the numbers and unlock the padlock!
- the number of dependent prepositions that follow a noun
- the number of dependent prepositions that follow an adjective
- the number of consonants in the name of the location

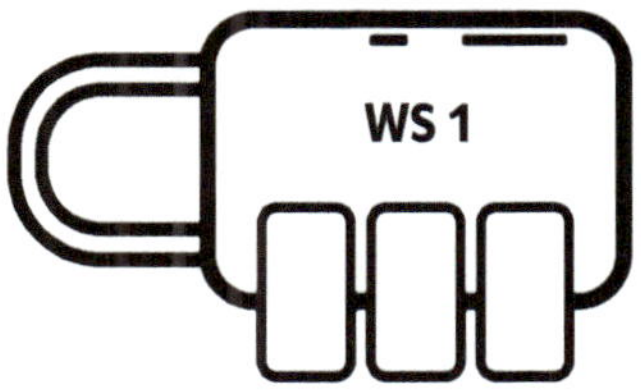

ISBN 978-3-12-506685-4

Clues used ✓		
①	②	③

Can you answer the questions?

Situation

Well done! You correctly guessed the location!

You are now outside the park with your friends. There is a **security officer** at the locked gates. There are a lot of fans, and they all want to meet Younes. The security officer agrees to let you in if you and your friends can solve a puzzle.

He gives one of you some questions and one of you some answers. First, can you add the missing prepositions? Then work with your partner to match the questions and answers. (Do not show each other your worksheets!)

security officer *Sicherheitsmitarbeiter*

Can you add the missing prepositions, and then match the questions to your partner's answers?

1 ◯ Which city was Younes raised .... ?

2 ◯ Did Younes get a degree .... art or film? Did he work .... videos at college?

3 ◯ What are the major influences .... Younes's style?

4 ◯ Do you think Younes's videos are popular .... everyone or are some people not fond .... his videos?

5 ◯ Do you think Younes is proud .... his success or does he have anxiety .... it?

6 ◯ How do you think Younes comes up .... his ideas .... his projects?

7 ◯ Imagine Younes invited you .... have a coffee. What would you say .... him?

What is the missing code? Write the numbers and unlock the padlock!

- the number of prepositions with two letters
- the number of prepositions that end with the letter *n*
- the number of prepositions that have more vowels than consonants

WS 2A

Edu Breakout Englisch – Escape Games für die 9./10. Klasse
ISBN 978-3-12-506685-4
Alles Digitale auf allango.net

Clues used ✓		
①	②	③

Can you answer the questions?

Situation

Well done! You correctly guessed the location!

You are now outside the park with your friends. There is a **security officer** at the locked gates. There are a lot of fans, and they all want to meet Younes. The security officer agrees to let you in if you and your friends can solve a puzzle.

He gives one of you some questions and one of you some answers. First, can you add the missing prepositions? Then work with your partner to match the questions and answers. (Do not show each other your worksheets!)

security officer *Sicherheitsmitarbeiter*

Can you add the missing prepositions, and then match the answers to your partner's answers?

A He is influenced .... street art and also his multicultural background. His family is from Morocco.

B I'd say thank you! Then I'd probably ask him .... his future plans. I'd also ask him how he deals .... criticism.

C I don't know. I think he's interested .... many different forms .... art. That's why we see so much variety .... his videos.

D He seems to be happy .... it. He has a reputation .... working hard, so he's probably very ambitious.

E He was raised .... Frankfurt in Germany.

F Well, he has over 50 million followers .... TikTok, so a lot of people like him! This number is similar .... his Instagram followers, too.

G No, but he studied .... the Provadis School .... International Management and Technology .... Frankfurt.

What is the missing code? Write the numbers and unlock the padlock!

- the number of prepositions that start with a consonant
- the number of prepositions that end with the letter *n*
- the number of prepositions that include the letter *o*

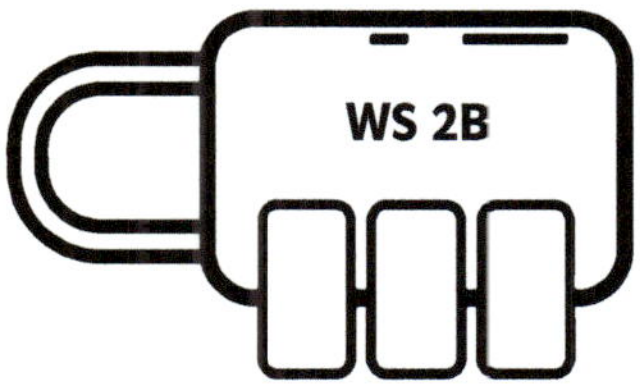

Alles Digitale auf allango.net
Edu Breakout Englisch – Escape Games für die 9./10. Klasse
ISBN 978-3-12-506685-4

How do you say ... ?

Can you solve the code?

Rationale

The students practise their reading and speaking skills to complete these puzzles. They also practise their writing and spelling skills in Worksheet 3.

Students practise and revise pronunciation patterns whilst exploring the sounds and lexis of tongue twisters in the context of an online game.

Situation

In Worksheet 1, students solve a puzzle to make tongue twisters.

In Worksheet 2A and 2B, students solve a code to find words for tongue twisters which they then take turns dictating to their partner.

Procedure

Worksheet 1: Set a time limit of three minutes for this task.

Differentiation

You can give groups who finish early, a related extension task.
For example:

- Worksheet 1: Students practise quietly saying the tongue twisters to themselves or write a tongue twister from their first language.
- Worksheet 2A and 2B: Students replace one word in each tongue twister with a suitable word or write their own tongue twisters.

Solutions

Worksheet 1

1 climb, cliff
2 proper, beside
3 sitting, shop
4 thirsty, feet
5 better, make

Worksheet 2A

1 fine, Thursday
2 shuffle *(schlurfen)*, share
3 witches, wish (**vicious** *gemein*)

Worksheet 2B

1 thick *(dumm)*, Tuesday
2 shamble *(watscheln)*, shake
3 violent, wait

Language focus

- pronunciation patterns

Codes & clues

WS 1 3 3 5
Clue 1
Each number represents one letter of the alphabet.

Clue 2
Each group of numbers represents one word.

Clue 3
When you find one letter in the code, look for the same number/letter in the other words – and write the letter there.

WS 2A and 2B 1 2 3
Clue 1
The six words are in the same order as the tongue twisters.

Clue 2
There is no gap between the words in the table.

Clue 3
Start with the letter in the top left square.

Clues used ✓		
①	②	③

Can you solve the code?

Situation

You are playing an online game with your friend. It's a new game about words, and you're now on Level 4. In this level, you have to solve a puzzle to make **tongue-twisters.**

tongue-twister *Zungenbrecher*

Can you use the code to complete the tongue twisters?

1 MAKE **2** SPEECH **3** OUT **4** AFTER **5** ESCAPE **6** BREAK **7** NOUNS
8 DAY **9** GAME **10** GERMANY **11** ADVERB **12** THOUSAND **13** TONGUE
14 SHOP **15** JOURNEY **16** ENGLISH **17** VILLAGE **18** BESIDE **19** AUSTRALIA

A How can I cleverly *5-16-19-9-11* a **craggy, crimson** *5-16-19-4-4?*

B A *2-15-13-2-10-15*, copper, coffee pot put *11-10-12-19-18-10* a proper potter's cup of coffee.

C I saw Sheila *12-19-3-3-19-7-17* in a shoe *12-14-13-2*. Where Sheila sits, she shines, and where Sheila shines, she sits.

D Thirty-thousand, *3-14-19-15-12-3-8*, **thundering thoroughbreds thumped** their *4-10-10-3* as they thundered through the **thorny thicket.**

E Betty bought some butter, but the butter Betty bought was bitter, so Betty bought some *11-10-3-3-10-15* butter to *9-6-1-10* the bitter butter better.

craggy *schroff* • **crimson** *rot* • **thundering** *donnernd* • **thoroughbred** *Vollblutpferd* • **to thump** *(auf)stampfen* • **thorny** *dornig* • **thicket** *Dickicht*

What is the missing code? Write the numbers and unlock the padlock!

- the number of verbs in the answers
- the number of nouns in the answers
- the number of answers with one syllable

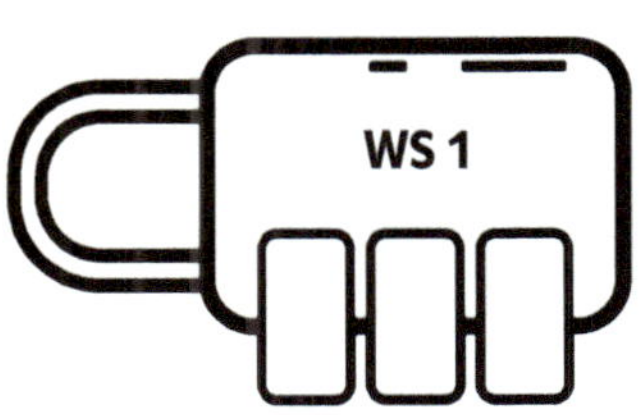

Edu Breakout Englisch –
Escape Games für die 9./10. Klasse
ISBN 978-3-12-506685-4

Clues used ✓		
①	②	③

Can you say the tongue twisters?

Situation

Well done! You solved the puzzle

You are now on Level 5. There is another code for you to solve, and then you have to work with a friend and dictate **tongue twisters**.

tongue twister *Zungenbrecher*

Can you find the six words to complete your tongue twisters?
Then take turns dictating your tongue twisters to your partner and writing their tongue twister. (Do not show each other your worksheets!)

F	I	N	E	T
H	U	R	S	D
A	Y	S	H	U
F	F	L	E	S
H	A	R	E	W
I	T	C	H	E
S	W	I	S	H

1 Thirteen .... thieves fought thirty-three thieves at the theatre for thinking about thumbs on ....

My partner: ....

....

2 Shy sheep .... swiftly and show sheer skill in shadowy grasses. How many shy sheep shall skilfully .... their shadows with their shepherd?

My partner: ....

....

3 If two vicious .... from two villages were watching two white watches, which witch from which village would .... to watch which white watch?

My partner: ....

....

What is the missing code? Write the numbers and unlock the padlock!

- the number of days in your tongue twisters
- the number of vowels in the first answer in item 2
- the number of answers in your tongue twisters with one syllable

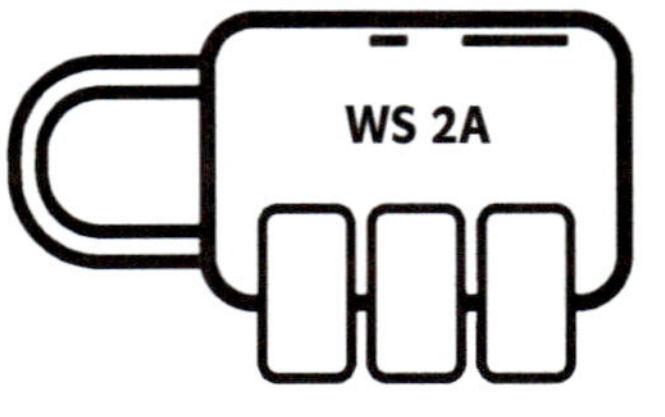

Edu Breakout Englisch – Escape Games für die 9./10. Klasse
ISBN 978-3-12-506685-4
Alles Digitale auf allango.net

Can you say the tongue twisters?

Clues used ✓		
①	②	③

Situation

Well done! You solved the puzzle

You are now on Level 5. There is another code for you to solve, and then you have to work with a friend and dictate **tongue twisters**.

tongue twister *Zungenbrecher*

Can you find the six words to complete your tongue twisters? Then take turns dictating your tongue twisters to your partner and writing their tongue twister. (Do not show each other your worksheets!)

T	H	I	C	K
T	U	E	S	D
A	Y	S	H	A
M	B	L	E	S
H	A	K	E	V
I	O	L	E	N
T	W	A	I	T

1 Thirteen .... thieves fought thirty-three thieves at the theatre for thinking about thrones on ....

My partner: ....

....

2 Shy sheep .... swiftly and show sheer skill in shadowy grasses. How many shy sheep shall skilfully .... their shadows with their shepherds?

My partner: ....

....

3 If two .... witches from two villages were watching two white watches, which witch from which village would .... to watch which white watch?

My partner: ....

....

What is the missing code? Write the numbers and unlock the padlock!

- the number of days in your tongue twisters
- the number of vowels in the first answer in item 2
- the number of answers in your tongue twisters with one syllable

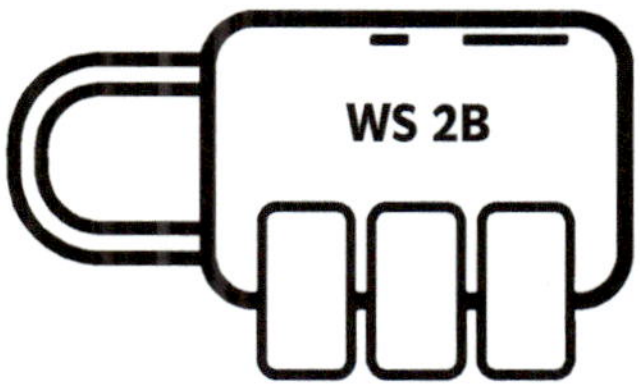

Music matters

Can you solve the puzzle?

Rationale

The students practise their reading and speaking skills to complete these puzzles. They also practise their basic writing skills.

Students practise and revise adverbial clauses for conditions (*even if, if, in case, only, if, unless*) through the context of music and visiting a concert hall.

Situation

In Worksheet 1, students solve a puzzle about different types of music. In Worksheet 2, students match descriptions of instruments. In Worksheet 3, students work out the missing words in someone's speech.

Differentiation

You can give groups who finish early, a related extension task. For example:

- Worksheet 1: Students write a definition for another type of music, art or film that they like.
- Worksheet 2: Students choose one instrument and write more information about it (true or imaginary) using some of the adverbial phrases.
- Worksheet 3: Students choose three (or more) of the adverbial phrases and use each in another sentence.

Solutions

Worksheet 1

1 Bollywood
2 Celtic music
3 Country music
4 Flamenco
5 K-Pop
6 Reggae

Worksheet 2

1C Drums
2A Harmonica
3E Didgeridoo
4D Flute
5B Harp

Worksheet 3

(1) only if
(2) Even if
(3) If
(4) unless
(5) in case

Language focus

- adverbial clauses of condition

Codes & clues

WS 1 L M G

Clue 1
Use each letter in the phrase 'From King BL' to fill in the gaps.

Clue 2
Use the letter *o* six times.

Clue 3
The types of music begin with *B, F, K* and *R*.

WS 2 9 8 6

Clue 1
Use *if* to introduce a general condition.

Clue 2
Use *only if* to introduce a requirement.
Use *even if* to introduce a fact and possibly a contradiction.

Clue 3
Use *unless* to introduce an exception.
Use *in case* to prepare for something.

WS 3 3 1 1

Clue 1
Use *if* to introduce a general condition.

Clue 2
Use *only if* to introduce a requirement.
Use *even if* to introduce a fact and possibly a contradiction.

Clue 3
Use *unless* to introduce an exception.
Use *in case* to prepare for something.

Clues used ✓		
①	②	③

Can you solve the puzzle?

Situation

You are on a school trip to a large concert hall in a nearby city. You are walking along an old corridor and listening to the tour guide. She explains that the main hall is closed due to a **rehearsal** for a **performance** tonight. You and your classmates are very excited about this, because the performance is actually a **gig** by one of your favourite bands.

You and your friends can hear the band playing, and you try to look through a small window in a door. There is a small note on the door.

rehearsal *Probe* • **performance** *Vorführung* • **gig** *Auftritt*

Can you solve the puzzle?

YOU CAN'T ENTER UNLESS YOU CAN SOLVE THE PUZZLE WITH THESE LETTERS: *FROM KING BL!*

1 _ _ _ _ yw_ _ d: You should watch some Indian films and practise your dancing in case you want to join in the amazing routines of this traditional Indian music.

2 Ce_t_c music: You may not like this music, unless you like Scottish bagpipes and Irish fiddles and flutes.

3 C_u_t_y music: If you're interested in everyday American life and love stories (usually sad ones), then you'll like this type of music.

4 _ _ a_e_c_: You'll love this type of music, but only if you like singing, dancing, playing the guitar and clapping your hands.

5 _-P_p: If you like pop music and want to learn more about South Korean culture, then you should listen to this.

6 _e_ _ ae: You'll enjoy this music and its message, even if Jamaican Bob Marley won't be singing.

What is the missing code? Write the numbers and unlock the padlock!

- the consonant that appears twice in answer 1
- the fourth letter in answer 4
- the consonant that appears twice in answer 6

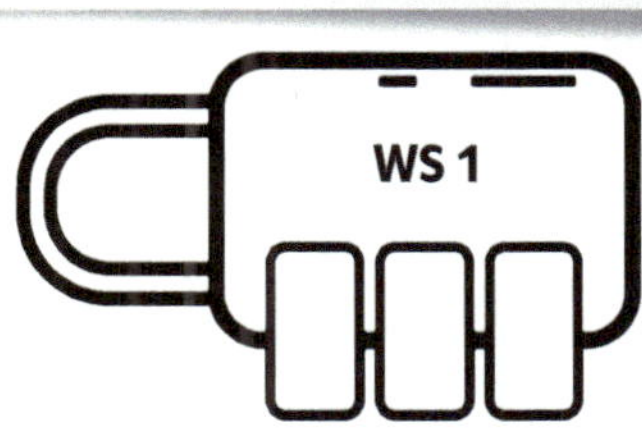

Clues used ✓		
①	②	③

Can you match the descriptions?

Situation

Well done! You solved the puzzle!

The door opens, and you enter the concert hall. It is **huge**! You start walking through the hall, but you see some musicians having an argument. Five of them are pulling a piece of paper **back and forth** between them. The paper rips. There are pieces of paper all over the ground. They have stopped arguing.

You ask if you can help. They explain that their instruments are in boxes, but the labels have disappeared. The piece of paper has the descriptions of each box, but the descriptions are now in pieces!

huge *riesig* • **back and forth** *hin und her*

Can you match the descriptions?

DIDGERIDOO | FLUTE | HARMONICA | DRUMS | HARP

A It isn't easy to carry instruments unless

B If you like large string instruments,

C You can learn to play with rhythm only if

D Even if you think woodwind instruments are boring,

E It's important to keep playing these in case

1 This is one of the easiest instruments to play, because you bang two sticks on its different parts. ______________________ you spend time practising your strokes and beats.

2 ______________________ you have one of these. It's small enough to fit inside your pocket and you play it with your mouth.

3 This is a very long instrument and reaches from the player's mouth down to the ground. ______________________ future generations start to forget their indigenous ancestors.

4 ______________________, you'll love this one. It's different because you hold it horizontally and blow into an opening.

5 ______________________, then you will like this one. It's a beautiful shape and you pluck the strings with your fingers.

What is the missing code? Write the numbers and unlock the padlock!

- the number of words in the phrase that matches item 1
- the number of words in the phrase that matches with item 3
- the number of words in the phrase that matches with item 5

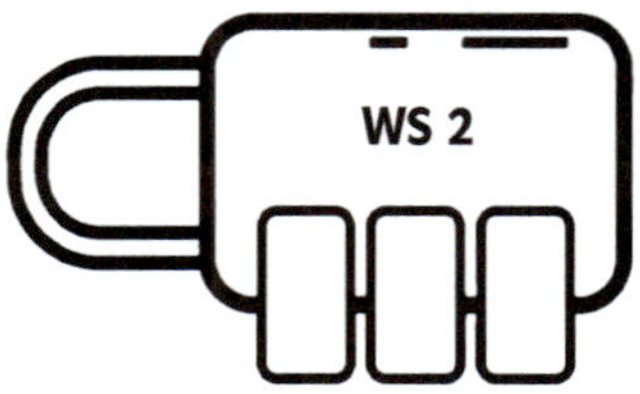

Edu Breakout Englisch – Escape Games für die 9./10. Klasse
ISBN 978-3-12-506685-4

Alles Digitale auf allango.net

Clues used ✓		
①	②	③

Can you find the missing words?

Situation

Well done! You matched the descriptions!

The musicians are very grateful, and they give you a special pass. You can go backstage! They point to a door by the stage. You are very excited and run to the door. The security guard stops you and talks on his radio. It's difficult to hear the other person … what are they saying?

Can you use your pass to find the missing words?

"Hello! I've checked with the boss. She said yes. They can go backstage, but (1) .... they have a pass. Do they have a pass? (2) .... they go backstage, they might not meet the band. It's a busy day today, and the band's schedule is full. (3) .... the band are rehearsing, then they can't talk to them. They can watch though. Remind them that they won't be able to stay for the concert (4) .... the band gives them tickets. Also, we need to contact their teacher (5) .... they miss the bus back to their school. Thanks!"

What is the missing code? Write the numbers and unlock the padlock!

- the number of times *if* is in the gaps
- the number of times *in* is in the gaps
- the number of times *only* is in the gaps

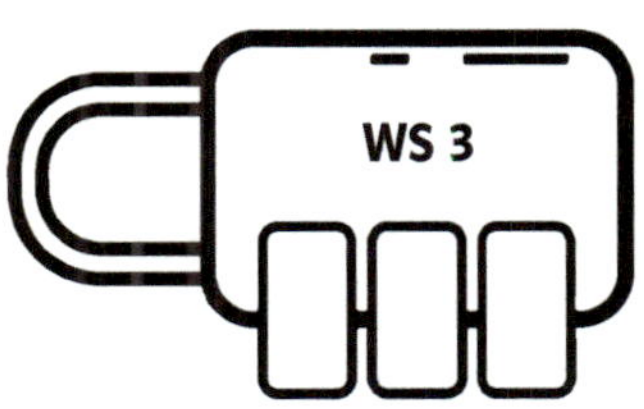

Edu Breakout Englisch –
Escape Games für die 9./10. Klasse
ISBN 978-3-12-506685-4

Puzzle club

Can you read the message?

Rationale
The students practise their reading and speaking skills to complete these puzzles. They also practise their basic writing skills and spelling.

Students practise and revise homophones and homographs through the context of taking part in a puzzle club competition.

Situation
In Worksheet 1, students solve a puzzle with numbers and words. In Worksheet 2, students work in pairs to identify (spell and say) seven pairs of homophones. In Worksheet 3, students complete a grid of homophones and homographs.

Differentiation
You can give groups who finish early, a related extension task. For example:
- Worksheet 1: Students choose three of the pairs of words and use both versions of the word in a new sentence.
- Worksheet 2: Students write a continuation of the story/dream using at least two pairs of words from Worksheet 2 (or Worksheet 1).
- Worksheet 3: Students look up and write example sentences for any new homographs or homophones in a grid.

Solutions

Worksheet 1	Worksheet 2	Worksheet 3
1 This message is for you: correct the bold words!	1 row	*(see / sea)*
2 aunt	2 row	*sell / cell*
3 read	3 object	write / right
4 cell	4 present	*knight / night*
5 two	5 wind	*son / sun*
6 meet	6 break	allowed / aloud
7 road	7 close	through / threw
8 sea	8 tear	their / there / they're
9 One	9 object	*deer / dear*
10 write	10 wind	***brake / break***
11 son	11 bow	*weather / whether*
12 weather	12 tear	know / no
13 some	13 break	***bear / bare***
14 seen	14 bow	flower / flour
15 Their	15 present	*tyre / tire*
16 whole	16 close	*principal / principle*
17 threw		*pear / pair*
		stare / stair

Language focus
- homophones
- homographs

Codes & clues

WS 1 6 2 4

Clue 1
For item 1, do the numbers look like letters of the alphabet?

Clue 2
Say the bold words aloud. What *other* words sound like the bold words?

Clue 3
Check the spelling of your answers matches the meaning of the word.

WS 2 2 1 1

Clue 1
The symbols are phonemes (sounds) and show you how to say the word.

Clue 2
Read the complete sentence and try to guess what type of word (e.g. noun or verb) is represented by the symbols.

Clue 3
All pairs of words have the same spelling.

WS 3 2 5 6

Clue 1
A homophone is a word that sounds the same as another word but has a different meaning and, often, a different spelling.

A homograph is a word that has the *same* spelling as another word but has a different meaning and/or pronunciation.

Clue 2
The verbs given in the grid are in the infinitve form.

Clue 3
There are 18 homophones and 12 homographs.

Can you read the message?

Clues used ✓		
①	②	③

Situation

It's Monday and that means it's puzzle club! You're really looking forward to it, because there is a competition today. The competition occurs every month and there are three rounds. The winner of each round is the person (or people) who completes the puzzle first.

You arrive and you **sign up** for round one.

sign up *sich einschreiben*

Can you read the message?

(1) 7H15 M3554G3 15 4 U: C0RR3C7 7H3 80LD W0RD5!

I got a book from my (2) **ant** and I (3) **red** it on my (4) sell. It's about (5) **too** people who (6) **meat** on a quiet (7) **rode** near the (8) **see.** (9) **Won** of them wants to (10) **right** a book. The other is looking for their (11) **sun.** They talk about the (12) **whether** and (13) **sum** of the strange things they have (14) **scene** in their lives. (15) **There** conversation was boring. The (16) **hole** book was boring. So, I (17) **through** it away.

1 ....

......................................!

2 ....

3 ....

4 ....

5 ....

6 ....

7 ....

8 ....

9 ....

10 ....

11 ....

12 ....

13 ....

14 ....

15 ....

16 ....

17 ....

What is the missing code? Write the numbers and unlock the padlock!

- the number of correct answers that end with a vowel
- the number of correct answers that have one consonant and two vowels
- the number of consonants in the correct answer for item 17

WS 1

ISBN 978-3-12-506685-4

Clues used ✓		
①	②	③

Can you find the homographs?

Situation

Well done! You read the message and corrected the words.

You're through to round two of the competition. It's a short story with seven pairs of **homographs**.

homograph *ein Wort, das gleich geschrieben wird, wie ein anderes, aber eine unterschiedliche Bedeutung hat und in manchen Fällen unterschiedlich ausgesprochen wird.*

Can you and your partner work together and identify (spell and say) the homographs?

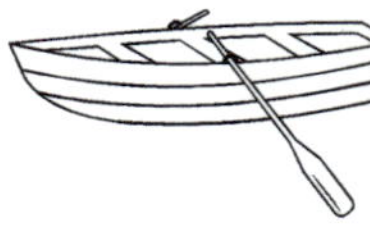

It had been a long journey. I had to (1) [rəʊ] the boat across a beautiful lake. When the boat was near the island, I could hear the loud angry voices of a (2) [raʊ]. One person was shouting "No, I (3) [ɒbˈdʒekt]! I will not give the king a (4) [ˈprezənt]!" Suddenly, the (5) [wɪnd] grew strong and blew the boat further along the island. I really needed a (6) [ˈbreɪk] when I finally saw the beach was (7) [kləʊs]. Finally!

I got to the beach and stepped out of the boat. There was a (8) [teə] in my trousers, but I was safe. Was I safe? There was a strange (9) [ˈɒbdʒɪkt] in the sand. It was an old watch. I tried to (10) [waɪnd] it up and then the face of a smiling man appeared before me. He wore a green (11) [bəʊ] in his hair and there was a single (12) [tɪə] on his cheek. He was on a unicycle and the wheel was about to (13) [ˈbreɪk].

There were more angry voices behind me, and the smiling man disappeared. I turned to see a group of people – one of them said "Go to our king! (14) [baʊ] before him and (15) [prɪˈzent] him with your gift. If you don't …" Then I heard a door (16) [kləʊs]. I opened my eyes … I was in my bed. It was all a dream!

(1) .... (2) .... (3) .... (4) .... (5) .... (6) .... (7) .... (8) ....

(9) .... (10) .... (11) .... (12) .... (13) .... (14) .... (15) .... (16) ....

What is the missing code? Write the numbers and unlock the padlock!

- the number of pairs of words that have two syllables
- the number of pairs of words that are both nouns
- the number of words that have only one short vowel sound

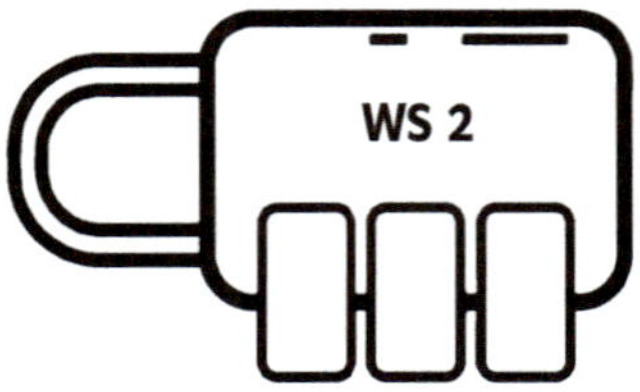

Edu Breakout Englisch – Escape Games für die 9./10. Klasse
ISBN 978-3-12-506685-4

Alles Digitale auf allango.net

Can you find the homophones?

Clues used ✓		
①	②	③

Situation

Well done! You and your partner identified the homographs!

You're through to the final round of the competition: homophone hunt!
Some of these words are **homophones** and some are homographs.

homophone *ein Wort, das gleich ausgesprochen wird wie ein anderes, aber eine andere Bedeutung hat und oft auch verschieden geschrieben wird*

How many homophones can you find that match the words given in the grid?

close	see sea	desert	sell	present ....
write	knight	object	read	son ....
tear	bow	allowed	row	through ....
their	deer	brake	weather	know ....
bear	flower	tyre	lead	minute ....
principal	invite	pear	wind	stare ....

What is the missing code? Write the numbers and unlock the padlock!

- the number of pairs of homophones with exactly the same letters
- the number of pairs of homographs that have two syllables
- the number of pairs of homophones that have at least two different letters

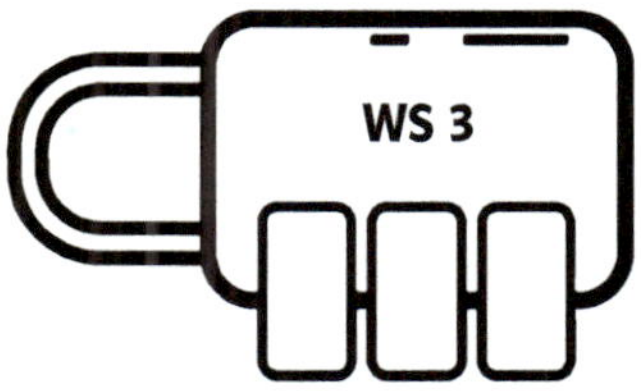

Alles Digitale auf allango.net

Edu Breakout Englisch – Escape Games für die 9./10. Klasse
ISBN 978-3-12-506685-4

Eat up!

Can you solve the puzzle?

Rationale

The students practise their reading and speaking skills to complete these puzzles. They also practise their basic writing skills.

Students practise and revise phrasal verbs through the context of international food and cooking.

Situation

In Worksheet 1, students solve a puzzle and complete a note about a recipe. In Worksheets 2A and 2B, students solve a puzzle to complete phrasal verbs and answer questions about international food, and then check their answers with their partner.

Differentiation

You can give groups who finish early, a related extension task. For example:

- Worksheet 1: Students write a reply to the note or students write a short recipe for a dish they enjoy.
- Worksheet 2A and 2B: Students choose (at least) three phrasal verbs from the ten on their and their partner's worksheets and use them in new sentences.

Solutions

Worksheet 1

1 written
2 clean
3 put
4 keep
5 heat
6 mix
7 Take
8 Round

A clean
B keep
C put
D round
E mix
F take
G write

Worksheet 2A

1 up c)
2 in b)
3 down a)
4 around b)
5 out of a)
Extra: on

Worksheet 2B

6 up with b)
7 up c)
8 down a)
9 in c)
10 from b)
Extra: on

Language focus

- phrasal verbs

Codes & clues

WS 1 **1 1 5**
Clue 1
There are 26 letters in the English alphabet.

Clue 2
What number relates to the letter 'A' in the example *clean*? What about 'C'?

Clue 3
Each number relates to the position of the letter in the English alphabet.

WS 2A **O W F**
Clue 1
Look at the puzzle in a different way … or use a mirror!

Clue 2
Phrasal verbs with *up* can mean increase or discover.

Clue 3
Phrasal verbs with *down* can mean decrease something by searching for one thing from a large choice or to do something quickly or enthusiastically.

WS 2B **N W I**
Clue 1
Look at the puzzle in a different way … or use a mirror!

Clue 2
Phrasal verbs with *up* can mean increase or discover.

Clue 3
Phrasal verbs with *down* can mean decrease something by searching for one thing from a large choice or to do something quickly or enthusiastically.

Clues used ✓		
①	②	③

Can you solve the puzzle?

Situation

It's the international food party at school this evening. This is one of your favourite events, because you get to try lots of different food. Everyone takes a **dish** they have made and which represents their country or culture. Your dad gives you a pasta recipe ... with a puzzle!

dish *Gericht*

Can you complete the note with the correct form of the verbs in the puzzle?

Hi Max,

I've (1) .... down the instructions for you. It's easy to make, but you'll need some verbs!

Can you (2) .... up after you've finished cooking? Please (3) .... away any food you didn't use.

Love,

Dad

A	3-12-5-1-14 = c l _ a _
B	11-5-5-16 = _ _ _ _
C	16-21-20 = _ _ _
D	18-15-21-14-4 = _ _ _ _ _ _
E	13-9-24 = _ _ _
F	20-1-11-5 = _ _ _ _
G	23-18-9-20-5 = _ _ _ _ _

Perfect Pasta

Boil water in a large pot. Add the pasta and cook for about eight minutes. Drain the spaghetti, but (4) .... back about 1/2 cup of pasta water.

While the pasta is cooking, gently (5 .... up some olive oil in a large pan. Add the garlic and (6) .... in the chilli pepper flakes. Sauté for 1–2 minutes or until the garlic is soft and golden.

Add the spaghetti to the pan and stir. (If the pasta looks dry, slowly pour in the pasta water until the consistency is better.)

(7) .... the pan off the heat. (8) .... off with salt and black pepper. Sprinkle chopped parsley and parmesan cheese on top.

What is the missing code? Write the numbers and unlock the padlock!

- the number of past participle verbs in the answers
- the number of phrasal verbs that have an object before their preposition
- the number of letters in answer 8

WS 1

Edu Breakout Englisch – Escape Games für die 9./10. Klasse
ISBN 978-3-12-506685-4

Clues used ✓		
①	②	③

Can you win the quiz?

Situation

Well done! You completed the note!

You arrive at the party with your food and look at all the different types of food on tables. It looks amazing!

Before eating, there is going to be a quiz for pairs of students. The winner gets a cookbook and a **voucher** for a café near the school. You and your friend really want to win …

voucher *Gutschein*

Can you complete the questions with prepositions from the box? (There is one extra preposition that you do not need!) Can you then answer the questions? Check your ideas with your partner.

quɈuoɟoninwobnobnuoɿɒ

1 Which Middle Eastern food consists of meat (usually lamb or beef) sliced .... into pieces and often eaten with flatbread?

(a) sushi (b) falafel (c) kebab

2 What would you indulge .... if you ate a model dish from Mexico?

(a) chicken (b) chocolate (c) rice

3 Which South American country loves to wolf .... grilled meat, especially beef?

(a) Argentina (b) Chile (c) Peru

4 Which country's traditional dish, 'haggis', is often passed .... the table to guests?

(a) Ireland (b) Scotland (c) Wales

5 If someone ran .... the main ingredient in the popular Brazilian dish 'feijoada', what food would be missing?

(a) beans (b) rice (c) quinoa

What is the missing code? Write the letters from YOUR answers and unlock the padlock!

- the first letter of the extra preposition
- the third letter of the preposition that completes the phrasal verb *wolf* ______
- the second letter of the second preposition in the three-part phrasal verb

WS 2A

Answers to questions 6–10 6 up with (b) 7 up (c) 8 down (a) 9 in (c) 10 from (b)

Edu Breakout Englisch – Escape Games für die 9./10. Klasse
ISBN 978-3-12-506685-4
Alles Digitale auf allango.net

Can you win the quiz?

Clues used ✓		
①	②	③

Situation

Well done! You completed the note!

You arrive at the party with your food and look at all the different types of food on tables. It looks amazing!

Before eating, there is going to be a quiz for pairs of students. The winner gets a cookbook and a **voucher** for a café school. You and your friend really want to win …

voucher *Gutschein*

Can you complete the questions with prepositions from the box? (There is one extra preposition that you do not need!) Can you then answer the questions? Check your ideas with your partner.

Hłiwququnimoɿłnonwob

6 Which country would you be in if you caught .... friends whilst having Pho noodles?

(a) China (b) Vietnam (c) Thailand

7 Which South Korean dish has been spiced .... but is also sweet?

(a) sushi (b) hummus (c) kimchi

8 In which country could you track .... a dish called 'Pad Tha'?

(a) Thailand (b) Indonesia (c) Malaysia

9 What is the key ingredient to put .... the Greek dish 'Spanakopita'?

(a) cheese (b) lamb (c) spinach

10 Which country does the sandwich originally come .... ?

(a) Germany (b) England (c) France

What is the missing code? Write the letters from YOUR answers and unlock the padlock!

- the second letter of the extra preposition
- the third letter of the preposition that completes the phrasal verb *track* ______
- the second letter of the second preposition in the three-part phrasal verb

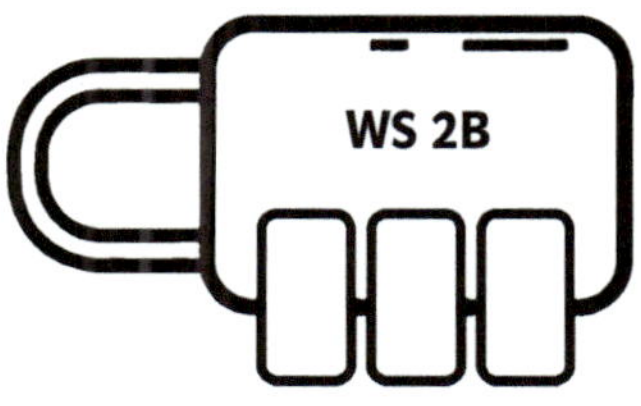

Answers to questions 1–5 1 up (c) 2 in (b) 3 down (a) 4 around (b) 5 out of (a)

Protecting the planet

Can you solve the code?

Rationale

The students practise their reading and speaking skills to complete these puzzles. They also practise their basic writing skills.

Students practise and revise adverbial clauses of contrast through the context of sustainability.

Situation

In Worksheet 1, students solve a code on a website. In Worksheet 2, students solve a riddle on the topic of sustainability. In Worksheet 3, students solve a puzzle and complete the tips.

Differentiation

You can give groups who finish early, a related extension task. For example:

- Worksheet 1: Students write (at least) two more sentences for the website.
- Worksheet 2: Students write a few sentences (or a simple riddle) about what their family or their school does to recycle.
- Worksheet 3: Students write more tips using the adverbs.

Solutions

Worksheet 1

1 though
2 While
3 Even though
4 Although
5 whereas

Worksheet 2

1 cycle
2 Though
3 While
4 Even though, continue
5 Although
6 Whereas
7 While
8 my
9 recycling

Worksheet 3

1C Though it may seem like an old message
2D even though they cost more than others
3A whereas individual vehicles result in greater pollution
4E Although everyone needs to take a shower
5B Even though this may not seem significant

Language focus

- adverbial clauses of contrast

Codes & clues

WS 1 T H S
Clue 1
Each symbol (!, %, and &) represents one letter.

Clue 2
You need all the letters in the code. You do not need any other letters.

Clue 3
Look for symbols that appear more than once. For example, *.

WS 2 C E G
Clue 1
Each line (_) and each blue square represent one missing letter.

Clue 2
Use the adverbs from Worksheet 1 to complete the riddle.

Clue 3
The nine letters in the boxes spell the missing word in item 9.

WS 3 8 7 4
Clue 1
Match the headings of tips 1–5 to the topics in A–E.

Clue 2
Adverbs are often the first word of the sentence or clause.

Clue 3
Use Subject-Verb-Object word order for the clauses.

Clues used ✓		
①	②	③

Can you solve the code?

Situation

Your favourite teacher is leaving your school, so you and your friends want to buy a gift for them. Your teacher has taught you about **sustainability** and how to protect the planet. You are looking online for a sustainable gift and you find an interesting website.

sustainability *Nachhaltigkeit*

Can you solve the code?

5% off for all NEW customers! Solve the code to get an EXTRA 15% off!

a	e	g	h	i	l	n	o	r	s	t	u	v	w
!	%	&	*	(	+	_	'	]	{	}	;	:	"

(We will add new customers to our mailing list,

(1) }*';&* .... you can opt out at any time.)

●●●

WELCOME TO ECO-NOW! THE ONLY DESTINATION FOR SUSTAINABLE FASHION!

(2) "*(+% .... fashion trends constantly develop, we prove that you can be stylish and eco-friendly!

(3) %:%_ }*';&* .... our clothes are at low prices, they are all made from natural and recycled materials!

(4) !+}*';&* .... you are buying something for yourself or a loved one, you are helping the planet. We make a donation to green charities for every purchase!

Many online shops do not offer climate-neutral shipping,

(5) "*%]%!{ .... we do! We deliver to your home or to your local pick-up point.

What is the missing code? Write the letters and unlock the padlock!

- the first letter in answer 1
- the fourth letter in answer 4
- the last letter in answer 5

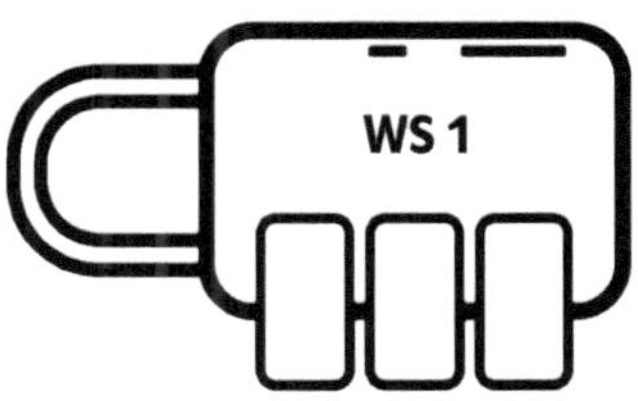

Edu Breakout Englisch – Escape Games für die 9./10. Klasse
ISBN 978-3-12-506685-4

Clues used ✓		
①	②	③

Can you solve the riddle?

Situation

Well done! You solved the code!

You choose a gift for your teacher and you get 5 % (and another 15 %) off. The gift has arrived at your local pick-up point and you go to collect it from the **locker**. There is a small screen and you scan the barcode from your email. A message appears on the screen.

locker *hier: Abholstation*

Can you write the missing letters and solve the riddle?

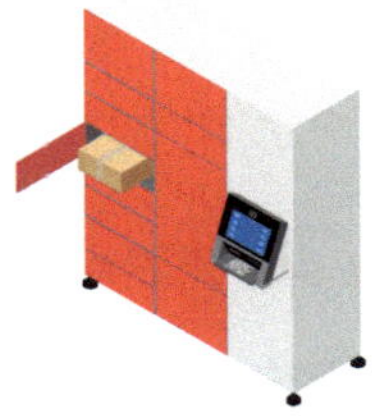

Solve the eco-riddle to unlock the locker and collect your Eco-Now parcel!

(1) In the cy [ ] le of life, I find my prime,

(2) Th_ _ [ ] h not new, my value does not decline.

(3) Wh_l [ ] some see waste, I see a chance,

(4) _v_ [ ] _h_ _gh I'm old, I [ ] ontinue to enhance.

(5) A [ ] th_ _gh not purchased, I'm rich in worth,

(6) Wh_ [ ] _ _s others reject, I find a re-birth.

(7) Wh [ ] l_ some things grow weak, I get better and shout,

(8) "What am I? Solve m [ ] riddle! What's it all about?"

This riddle is about (9) [ ] [ ] [ ] [ ] [ ] [ ] [ ] [ ] !

(Use the blue boxes to help you!)

What is the missing code? Put the letters from (9) in alphabetical order. Then write the first three letters and unlock the locker!

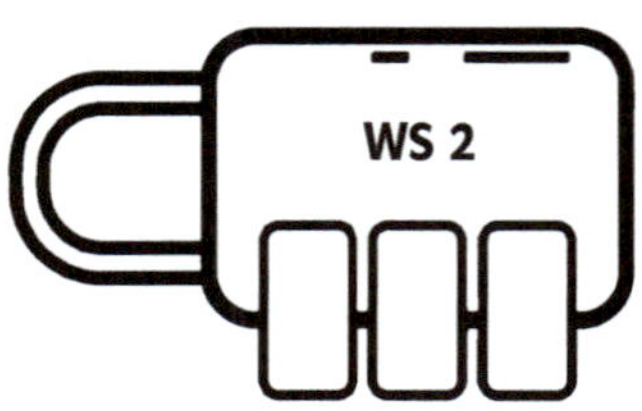

Edu Breakout Englisch – Escape Games für die 9./10. Klasse
ISBN 978-3-12-506685-4

Alles Digitale auf allango.net

Can you solve the puzzle?

Clues used ✓		
①	②	③

Situation

Well done! You solved the riddle!

You have now opened the locker and have the gift for your teacher. The gift is **wrapped** in recycled paper and there are words on it – it's a puzzle about sustainability tips.

to wrap *einpacken*

Can you put the words in the correct order and then add them to the correct tip below?

A greater | individual vehicles | pollution | result in | whereas

B seem | even though | may not | this | significant

C an old | it may | seem like | though | message

D cost | even though | more than | they | others

E a shower | to take | needs | everyone | although

FIVE SUSTAINABILITY TIPS

1 Reduce, Reuse, Recycle – ....
these actions still have long-lasting effects. Reduce what you use, reuse whenever possible, and recycle materials such as paper, plastic, and glass.

2 Save Energy – Turn off lights and devices when you are not using them, and unplug any chargers, too.
Use energy-efficient light bulbs, ...

3 Use Public Transport – While it may be more convenient to travel by car, try using public transportation or cycling for shorter journeys. Public transport produces fewer emissions compared to multiple individual vehicles, ...

4 Save Water – .... ,
try to save water by taking less time. We can also save water by turning off the tap when we brush teeth or wash dishes after a meal. Rainwater can also be collected and used for plants.

5 Educate Others – Share your knowledge with your friends and family. Encourage them to adopt your habits to protect the environment and listen to their ideas. .... ,
you could learn a lot and have a more positive impact on the planet.

What is the missing code? Write the letters and unlock the padlock!

- the number of words in the answer to tip 1
- the number of letters in the adverb in the answer to tip 3
- the number of syllables in the longest word in the answer to tip 5

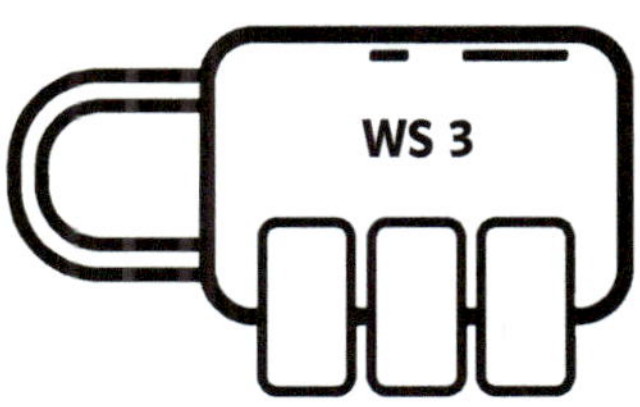

ISBN 978-3-12-506685-4

Alphabet Adventure

Can you find the answers?

Rationale

The students practise their reading and speaking skills to complete these puzzles. They also practise their basic writing skills.

Students practise and revise *would* and *used to* through the context of alphabets and Old English.

Situation

In Worksheet 1, students choose the correct answers to complete a history about alphabets. In Worksheet 2A and 2B, students solve a code and add verbs to information about the Old English alphabet.

Differentiation

You can give groups who finish early, a related extension task. For example:

- Worksheet 1: Students cover their worksheet and write a few sentences describing the history of the alphabet.
- Worksheet 2A and 2B: Students use the information in the texts or their own knowledge to write sentences using *would* and *used to* about alphabets or languages.

Solutions

Worksheet 1

1 would
2 to
3 would
4 used to
5 didn't

Worksheet 2A

1 didn't use to have
2 used to represent, significance
3 used to have, swords
4 historical

Worksheet 2B

1 used to write
2 used to believe, spiritual
3 would show, warriors
4 popularity

Language focus

- *would* and *used* to

Codes & clues

WS 1 w o i
Clue 1
Do not use to after *would.*

Clue 2
Use and *used to* have different meanings – to employ something for a purpose and to describe past repeated actions.

Clue 3
Use *not* + *use to* to make the negative form of used to.

WS 2A and 2B e e u
Clue 1
The stones show our alphabet and the equivalent letter in the Old English alphabet.

Clue 2
Read the complete text first to understand the main ideas.

Clue 3
Look at the words before and after the gap. What verbs might suit the context?

Clues used ✓		
①	②	③

Can you find the answers?

Situation

You are in the park with your friend. You see a small bag by a rock. Your friend picks it up – there's an old watch inside. You look at the watch. The **hands** start moving backwards and turn faster and faster … where are you? You're both confused. You're not in the park anymore. You're standing next to some pyramids!

Your friend looks in the bag again and pulls out a sheet of old paper.

hand *Zeiger*

Can you find the answers?

Welcome to the history of the alphabet – you're in ancient Egypt! You can go home if you can find the correct answers.

In the past, our **ancestors** (1) .... *(made/would/used)* use symbols to communicate with others.

'Hieroglyphs' were among the earliest ways people used (2) .... *(for/in/to)* 'write'. This is dated around 3200 BCE. People would **carve** the stones of a pyramid or make pictures on papyrus to represent objects, sounds, and ideas.

The 'Harappan' script was used by the (3) Indus Valley Civilisation from about 3300 to 1300 BCE. They (3) .... *(did/used/would)* make symbols on pottery and **seals**. The script still hasn't been decoded.

Writing in China started during the Shang dynasty, which (4) .... *(used/would/used to)* exist around 1600–1046 BCE. Early characters used to look like pictures, but these gradually changed over time.

The Phoenicians created one of the first alphabets in around 1050 BCE. It used to have 22 letters. Perhaps surprisingly, vowels (5) .... *(didn't/hadn't/weren't)* use to be represented in this alphabet – there were no symbols for vowels!

ancestors *Vorfahren* • **to carve** *einritzen* • **seal** *Siegel*

What is the missing code? Write the numbers and unlock the padlock!

- the first letter in the correct answer to item 1
- the final letter in the correct answer to item 4
- the second letter in the correct answer to item 5

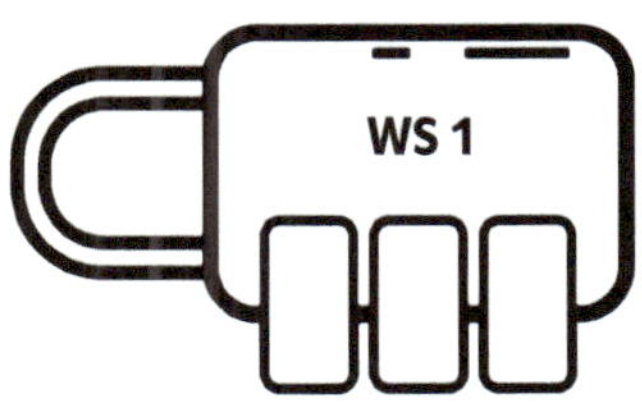

Edu Breakout Englisch – Escape Games für die 9./10. Klasse
ISBN 978-3-12-506685-4

Clues used ✓		
①	②	③

Can you solve the puzzle?

Situation

Well done! You found the correct answers!

You look at the watch again and the hands start turning faster and faster … and now you're back in the park! You want to go on another alphabet adventure, so you shake the watch a few times. Nothing happens. You put it back in the bag and then you feel something else in the bag. There are two sheets of paper: one for you and one for your friend. There are nine stones, too.

Can you solve the puzzle … and then add the verbs? Check your ideas with your partner.

used to have

used to represent

S = ᛋ

didn't use to have

W = ᚻ

N = ᚾ

O = ᚩ

I = ᛁ

A = ᚨ

(1) Long ago, our ancestors .... the internet or emails! If they wanted to make any written statement, they used to write symbols on objects like walls, stones or even weapons.

(2) The symbols in the bag are from an Old English alphabet and they are called 'runes'. Runes weren't just .... letters and make words though. People used to believe that the runes had spiritual ᛋᛁgᚾᛁfᛁcᚨᚾce and possessed special qualities.

(3) Back in those times, people would cut the runes (or the symbols) onto various objects with a sharp tool. These runes would show ownership or a wish for good fortune. For example, warriors .... runes into their ᛋᚻᚩrdᛋ before a battle.

(4) This fascinating alphabet began to decline with the popularity of the Latin alphabet, though runes can still be seen on some hᛁᛋtᚩrᛁcᚨl objects. It can be easy to forget how our ancestors would have used it all the time – it was their tool for written communication.

What is the missing code? Write the numbers and unlock the padlock!

- the final letter of the main verb in answer 1
- the second letter of the main verb in answer 2
- the third letter of the modal verb in answer 3

WS 2A

Answers for 2B (1) used to write (2) used to believe, spiritual (3) would show, warriors (4) popularity

Edu Breakout Englisch – Escape Games für die 9./10. Klasse
ISBN 978-3-12-506685-4
Alles Digitale auf allango.net

Can you solve the puzzle?

Clues used ✓		
①	②	③

Situation

Well done! You found the correct answers!

You look at the watch again and the hands start turning faster and faster … and now you're back in the park! You want to go on another alphabet adventure, so you shake the watch a few times. Nothing happens. You put it back in the bag and then you feel something else in the bag. There are two sheets of paper: one for you and one for your friend. There are nine stones, too.

Can you solve the puzzle … and then add the verbs? Check your ideas with your partner.

used to believe

used to write

S = ᛋ

would show

W = ᚻ

N = ᚾ

O = ᚩ

I = ᛁ

A = ᚨ

(1) Long ago, our ancestors didn't use to have the internet or emails! If they wanted to make any written statement, they .... symbols on objects like walls, stones or even weapons.

(2) The symbols are from an Old English alphabet, and they are called 'runes'. Runes weren't just used to represent letters and make words though. People .... that the runes had ᛋpᛁrᛁtuᚨl significance and possessed special qualities.

(3) Back in those times, people would cut the runes (or the symbols) onto various objects with a sharp tool. These runes .... ownership or a wish for good fortune. For example, ᚻᚨrrᛁᚩrᛋ used to have runes cut into their swords before a battle.

(4) This fascinating alphabet began to decline with the pᚩpulᚨrᛁty of the Latin alphabet, though runes can still be seen on some historical objects. It can be easy to forget how our ancestors would have used it all the time – it was their tool for written communication.

What is the missing code? Write the numbers and unlock the padlock!

- the final letter of the main verb in answer 1
- the second letter of the main verb in answer 2
- the third letter of the modal verb in answer 3

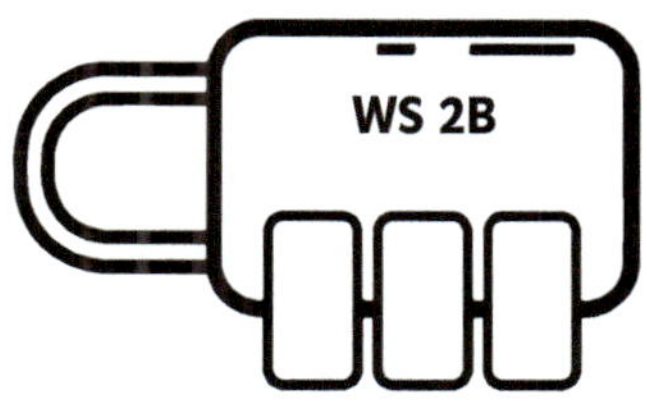

Answers for 2A (1) didn't use to have to have, swords (2) used to represent, significance (4) historical (3) used

Eco Mission

Can you complete the puzzle?

Rationale

The students practise their reading and speaking skills to complete these puzzles. They also practise their basic writing skills.

Students practise and revise participle constructions through the context of environmental issues.

Situation

In Worksheet 1, students make sentences (with participle constructions) from words on placards. In Worksheet 2, students fix a blog by adding the correct form of the verbs to blog titles. In Worksheet 3, students correct grammatical errors in a draft blog.

Differentiation

You can give groups who finish early, a related extension task. For example:

- Worksheet 1: Students choose a beginning of (at least) one of the sentences and write a different ending.
- Worksheet 2: Students choose one of the blog topics and write a short paragraph on the topic.
- Worksheet 3: Students write their own positive statements about environmental matters using (at least) two of the verbs in the answers or their own ideas.

Solutions

Worksheet 1

1 **Before** voting, ask your politician for their views!
2 Instead of doing nothing, we demand our politicians act **now**!
3 Knowing our planet's in danger, we stand together **today**!
4 **Starting** today, we need action from our government!

Worksheet 2

(1) Disappointed
(2) Having brought
(3) Being
(4) Not being
(5) Resulting
(6) Causing

Worksheet 3

(1) Committed
(2) Using *(is correct)*
(3) Encouraged
(4) Reacting
(5) By choosing
(6) While volunteering
(7) Since supporting
(8) Having participated

Language focus

- participle constructions

Codes & clues

WS 1 2 6 4

Clue 1
Participle constructions usually begin with a participle form of the verb (present, past or perfect).

Clue 2
Participle constructions can begin with a conjunction, e.g. *before* or *instead of.*

Clue 3
Participle constructions are usually followed by the subject and the main verb.

WS 2 1 4 1

Clue 1
Read the complete blog title. Which verb would be suitable for the topic?

Clue 2
Look at the prepositions after the gap. Which verbs go before these prepositions?

Clue 3
Look at the tense of the main verb in the second clause. Which tense do you need for the missing verb?

WS 3 2 5 1

Clue 1
Participle constructions can have different participle forms of the verb, i.e. present, past or perfect.

Clue 2
Look at the tense of the main verb in the second clause. Which is the best tense for the participle form of the verb?

Clue 3
The *-ing* form of the verb often follows conjunctions or prepositions.

Can you complete the puzzle?

Clues used ✓		
①	②	③

Situation

You are on the bus and on the way to meet your friend in the city centre. Suddenly, the bus stops, and the driver asks everyone to get off. You look out the window and see that there is a large crowd of **protestors** blocking the road. The people at the front are holding **placards** which have one word on them, so that together the placards make a sentence. They refuse to let you through … but then you tell them their placards are in the wrong order and you offer to help

protestor *Demonstranten* • **placard** *Plakat*

Can you make sentences from the words?

1 **BEFORE** .... **!**

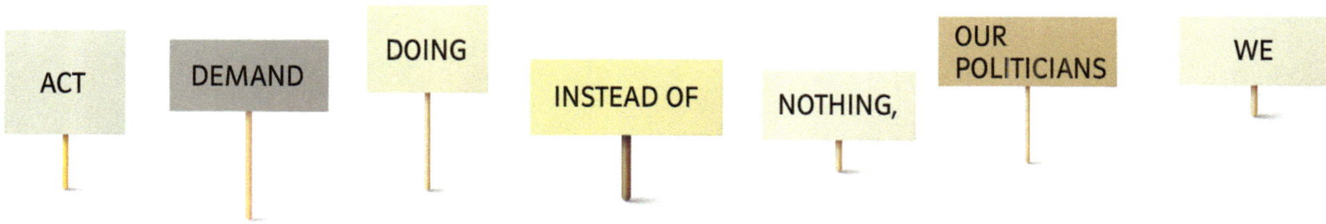

2 .... **now!**

3 .... **today!**

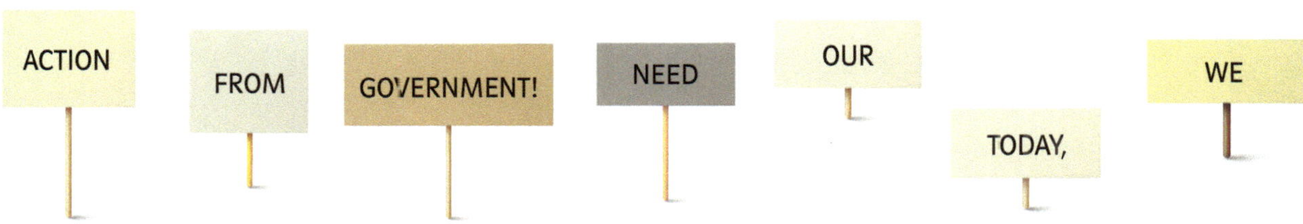

4 **STARTING** .... **!**

What is the missing code? Write the numbers and unlock the padlock!

- the number of sentences with a preposition or conjunction before the participle
- the number of words after the comma in answer 1
- the number of words before the comma in answer 2

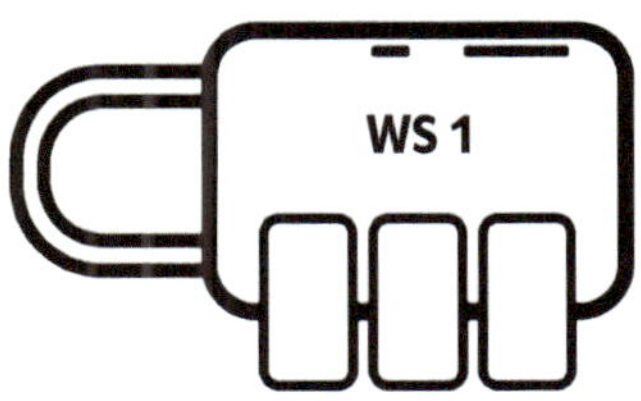

Edu Breakout Englisch – Escape Games für die 9./10. Klasse
ISBN 978-3-12-506685-4

Clues used ✓		
①	②	③

Can you fix the blogs?

Situation

Well done! You helped the protestors make sentences!

They are grateful and let you pass through the blocked road. One of them, Blake, helps you pass through the crowd to the other side of the road. You talk about the protest and Blake tells you about his new blog. He needs someone to fix a technical error, as the first word of each blog title is missing. You are good at **coding** and offer to help again.

coding *programmieren*

Can you add the correct form of the verbs to the blog titles?

BLOG TITLES

SYSTEM FAILURE
Error report: *be*
Error report: *bring*
Error report: cause
Error report: *disappoint*
Error report: *not be*
Error report: *result*

Click to read the complete blog!

1 .... by our government's lack of progress, we organised protests around the country to unite people and to demand action.

2 .... about damage in the past, we must change our behaviour now and protect the future of our planet.

3 .... the major greenhouse gas responsible for global warming, carbon dioxide CO_2 is a significant concern for environmentalists.

4 .... a renewable source of energy, nuclear power does not offer any sustainable solutions to energy needs.

5 .... from logging, deforestation is killing many natural habitats and species of plant and animal.

6 .... harm to marine life and potentially human life, water pollution continues to be an area of scientific and legal investigation.

What is the missing code? Write the numbers and unlock the padlock!

- the number of past participles in the answers
- the number of present participles in the answers
- the number of perfect participles in the answers

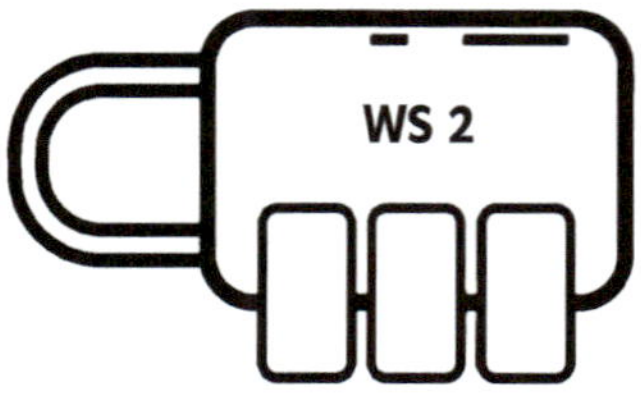

Edu Breakout Englisch – Escape Games für die 9./10. Klasse
ISBN 978-3-12-506685-4

Alles Digitale auf allango.net

Can you correct the errors?

Clues used ✓		
①	②	③

Situation

Well done! You fixed the blog titles!

Then you see your friend and introduce them to Blake. They get on well and you all have a long conversation about the planet. You begin to feel sad, but Blake tells you that there are many reasons to be positive. He shows you a draft of his new blog. There are some errors too, but these are grammatical ones.

Can you correct the grammatical errors? There is one correct participle construction.

BLOG TITLES

Click to read the complete blog!

1. ***Committing*** .... to making a change, we made a list of the different ways people and organisations can make a difference.
2. ***Using*** .... energy-efficient appliances such as kettles, toasters or washing machines, individuals can effectively and easily reduce their carbon footprint.
3. ***Having encourage*** .... by the popularity of solar power, many homeowners are choosing to install solar panels on roofs.
4. ***Reacted*** .... to consumers' concerns, many companies have a sustainability statement on their websites which details their approach to packaging, energy use and other matters.
5. ***By chosen*** .... public transport or carpooling, commuters can reduce air pollution and ease traffic congestion.
6. ***While volunteered*** .... for litter picks, you may meet many interesting people and learn about other local schemes.
7. ***Since supported*** .... eco-friendly businesses, many people feel they can make ethical choices when buying goods.
8. ***Having participating*** .... in community gardens, people have experienced the positive impact of green spaces and working with others.

What is the missing code? Write the numbers and unlock the padlock!

- the number of past participles in the answers
- the number of present participles in the answers
- the number of perfect participles in the answers

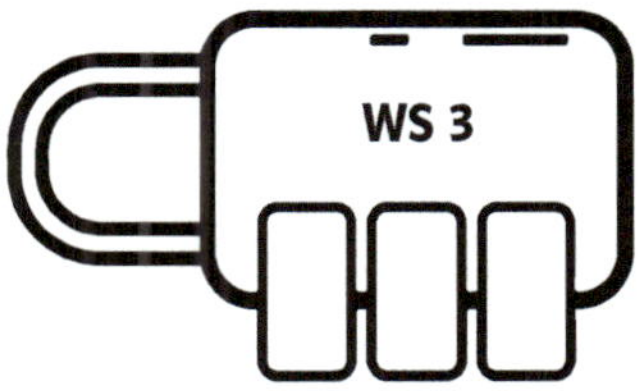

ISBN 978-3-12-506685-4

Which city?

Can you solve the puzzle?

Rationale
The students practise their reading and speaking skills to complete these puzzles. They also practise their basic writing skills.

Students practise and revise conditional clauses through the context of travel to other cities.

Situation
In Worksheet 1, students solve a word puzzle to answer questions about London. In Worksheet 2, students choose the correct missing words from questions and sentences about London. In Worksheet 3, students solve a crossword puzzle about English-speaking capital cities.

Situation
You can give groups who finish early, a related extension task. For example:
- Worksheet 1: Students write other facts about London as quiz questions or standard sentences.
- Worksheet 2: Students write (at least) two more sentences that the mechanic might say.
- Worksheet 3: Students write (at least) three more sentences about their own capital city or another capital city.

Solutions

Worksheet 1
(1) Elizabeth, Big Ben
(2) London Eye, Thames
(3) Trafalgar, National
(4) cathedral, Paul's

Worksheet 2
1 would have seen
2 take
3 can have
4 would go
5 could watch
6 would have got

Worksheet 3
1 Ottawa
2 Washington
3 Cape Town
4 New Delhi
5 Nassau
6 Kingston
7 Wellington
8 Nairobi

Language focus
- conditional clauses

Codes & clues

WS 1 1 0 0
Clue 1
Each square contains the nine letters of the missing word in the question.

Clue 2
The missing word in each question begins with the letter in the middle of the square.

Clue 3
The answers to the questions include these letter combinations: *ation*, *aul*, and *ham*.

WS 2 5 1 3
Clue 1
We form the zero conditional with present simple + present simple. We form the first conditional with present simple + *will/won't* + verb.

Clue 2
We form the second conditional with past simple + *would* + verb, and the third conditional with past perfect + *would have* + past participle.

Clue 3
We can replace *will* and *would* with other modals like *can* and *could*.

WS 3 2 2 2
Clue 1
The cities in the first conditional sentences are Kingston and Cape Town.

Clue 2
The cities in the second conditional sentences are Ottawa and Nassau.

Clue 3
The cities in the third conditional sentences are New Delhi and Wellington.

Can you solve the puzzles?

Clues used ✓		
①	②	③

Situation

You are walking home having spent the afternoon with your friends. You notice a small pathway between two buildings. There is an old, metal gate and it is open. What's down there? You've never noticed this pathway before. You walk slowly down the pathway and through the gate.

You are no longer on a path. You are in a small, **brightly-lit** laboratory with a large screen. There are four puzzles on the screen and a loud alarm is **going off**. A man is standing in front of the screen. He sees you and points at the screen. It looks like he needs your help. Can you solve the puzzles and stop the alarm?

brightly-lit *hell erleuchtet* • **to go off** *losgehen*

Can you find the missing words in the puzzles … and then answer the questions?

1

B	L	A
I	E	T
E	Z	H

Q: If you are in the … Tower, what famous clock are you very close to?

A: B_ _. B _ _ .

2

O	E	N
O	L	D
N	Y	E

Q: If you were on the …, which river would you be able to see?

A: The River T _ _ _ e s .

3

A	G	R
R	T	A
A	L	F

Q: Which gallery would you be near if you went to … Square?

A: The N_ _ _ _ _ a l Gallery

4

R	E	A
H	C	A
L	D	T

Q: Where would you be if you were in a … that was rebuilt after the Great Fire of London in 1666?

A: Saint P_ _ _ 's .

What is the missing code?
Add together the total number of vowels in the ANSWERS to the four questions and times by 10 … and unlock the padlock!

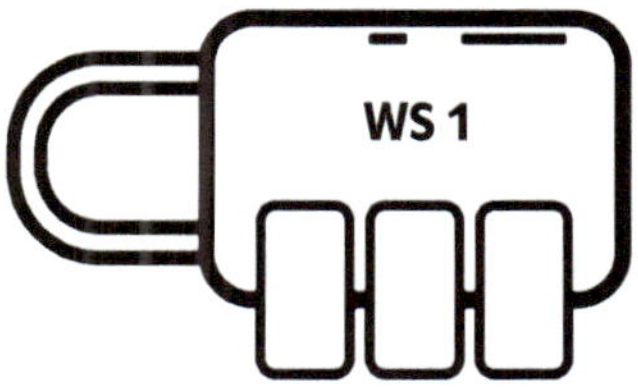

Edu Breakout Englisch – Escape Games für die 9./10. Klasse
ISBN 978-3-12-506685-4

Clues used ✓		
①	②	③

Can you find the correct notes?

Situation

Well done! You solved the puzzles and stopped the alarm!

The man introduces himself. His name is Husain, and he is a pilot. The small room is actually the inside of his flying machine. He needs to go to London **urgently**, so that a mechanic can fix a problem with the machine. He also needs an assistant for the trip … and he asks you to take the role. You say yes.

Husain presses a button. There is a strange **whistling** sound, and then Husain says, "Welcome to London!"

A mechanic enters the room and immediately starts work. Husain asks you to listen and write down what the mechanic says. He gives you some notes to help you.

urgently *dringend* • **whistling** *Pfeifen*

Can you complete the mechanic's questions and sentences with the correct notes? There are six extra notes you do not need.

can watch

can have

1 If you had visited London back in 2012, you .... the Olympics.

2 Are you going outside? It might rain later, ... an umbrella.

go

could watch

4 I would love to be a pilot. If I were a pilot, I ...... to Canada.

3 If the weather improves, you .... a picnic in Hyde Park.

have got

see

had

6 If you had contacted me earlier, I .... you tickets for the London Eye!

5 If you had more time here, you .... a West End show.

take

will take

would have got

would go

would have seen

What is the missing code? Write the numbers and unlock the padlock!

- the number of irregular past participles in the correct notes
- the number of regular past participles in the correct notes
- the number of correct notes with two words

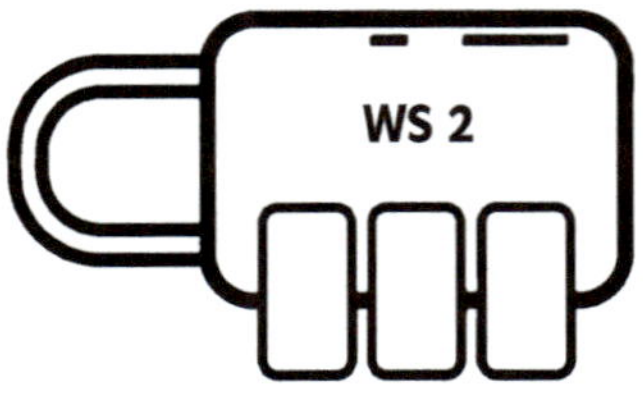

Edu Breakout Englisch – Escape Games für die 9./10. Klasse
ISBN 978-3-12-506685-4

Alles Digitale auf allango.net

Can you complete the puzzle?

Clues used ✓		
①	②	③

Situation

Well done! You completed the mechanic's questions and sentences!

The machine is fixed and the mechanic leaves. Husain asks if you'd like to visit another city on the way home and gives you a list of possible **destinations**. You would love to go to all of them, so Husain makes you a promise. If you can solve this puzzle, then he will take you to all of the cities!

destination *Ziel*

Can you solve the clues and complete the puzzle?

DOWN

1. **Canada flag** If you were in a city known for Parliament Hill and a river with the same name as the city, you would be in …
2. **USA** If you are in a city with a very famous white house, you are probably in …
4. **India** If you had experienced the busy market of Chandni Chowk, you would have visited …
6. **Jamaica** If you want a city with a rich history of reggae music, you won't be disappointed with …

ACROSS

3. **South Africa** If you want to see the Atlantic Ocean and a mountain named after a table, you will love …
5. **Bahamas** If you were surrounded by stunning beaches and coral reefs, you would probably be in the city of …
7. **New Zealand** If you had heard the sound of a traditional Maori haka, you would have travelled to …
8. **Kenya** If you find yourself in a city full of wild animals and safari adventures, you might be in …

What is the missing code? Write the numbers and unlock the padlock!

- the number of sentences with the zero conditional
- the number of capital cities with two words
- the number of sentences with the third conditional

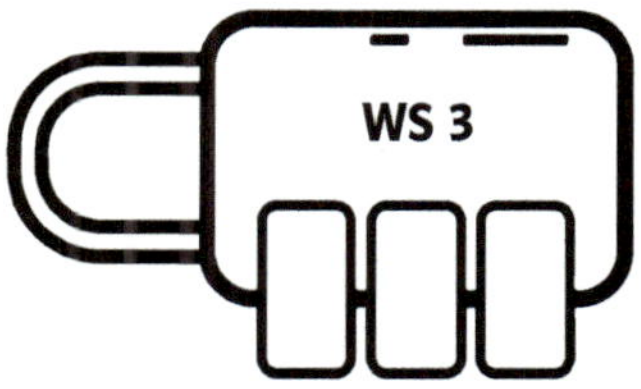

ISBN 978-3-12-506685-4

Eco exhibition

Can you solve the puzzle?

Rationale

The students practise their reading and speaking skills to complete these puzzles. They also practise their basic writing skills.

Students practise and revise adverbial clauses of time through the context of attending an environmental exhibition.

Situation

In Worksheet 1, students solve a puzzle about an environmental exhibition. In Worksheet 2A and 2B, students complete sentence beginnings and then work together to match sentence halves.

Differentiation

You can give groups who finish early, a related extension task. For example:

- Worksheet 1: Students use the code to write a sentence about themselves or the environment.
- Worksheet 2A and 2B: Students use the adverbial phrases of time to write more sentences about themselves or the environment.

Solutions

Worksheet 1

1 As soon as
2 the time
3 Once
4 Since
5 Until
6 When
7 Whenever
8 After

Worksheet 2A

1 species H
2 pollution F
3 plastic J
4 environmental I
5 natural G

Worksheet 2B

6 climate B
7 conservation E
8 habitats A
9 extreme C
10 damage D

Language focus

- adverbial clauses of time

Codes & clues

WS 1 1 2 1
Clue 1
Each symbol represents two letters.

Clue 2
There are five vowels in the English alphabet: *a, e, i, o,* and *u*.

Clue 3
There are 21 consonants in the English alphabet, such as *b, c,* and *d* at the beginning through to *x, y,* and *z* at the end.

WS 2A 6 7 3
Clue 1
Before indicates a time earlier than another event. *After* indicates a time following another event. *When* indicates the time something happens. *Whenever* indicates something that happens repeatedly.

Clue 2
As soon as indicates something will happen immediately after another event. *By the time* indicates when an action or event will be completed.

Clue 3
Once indicates something will happen after a particular event. *Since* indicates an event that continues from that time onwards. *Until* indicates the time up to which an action continues.

WS 2B 2 4 6
Clue 1
Before indicates a time earlier than another event. *After* indicates a time following another event. *When* indicates the time something happens. *Whenever* indicates something that happens repeatedly.

Clue 2
As soon as indicates something will happen immediately after another event. *By the time* indicates when an action or event will be completed.

Clue 3
Once indicates something will happen after a particular event. *Since* indicates an event that continues from that time onwards. *Until* indicates the time up to which an action continues.

Clues used ✓		
①	②	③

Can you solve the puzzle?

Situation

You are working on a project about the environment at school. Today, you are on a school trip to an exhibition about the climate crisis. There is a very long queue to enter the building, and you are feeling bored and cold. The exhibition opens in about five minutes.

Then everyone in the queue starts talking excitedly, and your teacher tells you about a competition. Each day, the organisers of the exhibition create a new puzzle for visitors. The first visitor to solve the puzzle is the first visitor to enter the exhibition that day, and they win a VIP pass and a bag full of prizes. Your teacher gives you and your friends the puzzle.

Can you solve the puzzle?

@ a + consonant

vowel + n

? wh

* ce

% he

> ti

ə er

(1) **_ _(@) so_ _(#) _ _(@)** visitors step inside the exhibition, they are transported into a world of environmental wonders: the journey begins, and they observe the impact of human activity on ecosystems.

By (2) **t_ _(%) _ _me(>)** they reach the interactive displays, a deep understanding of the climate has begun to develop.

(3) **_ _ _ _(#*)** immersed in the exhibits, visitors witness the reality of climate change.

(4) **S _ _ _ _ (#*)** the industrial revolution, our planet has suffered dramatic changes.

(5) **_ _ _ _l(#>) now,** many visitors may not have realised the urgency of the situation.

(6) **_ _ _ _(?#)** exploring the section on renewable energy, visitors experience some hope for the future.

(7) **_ _ _ _ev_ _(?#ə)** visitors learn of ways to help our planet and want to help our planet, we feel the exhibition has been a success.

(8) **_ _t_ _(@ə)** leaving the exhibition, visitors feel a strong commitment to look after our environment.

What is the missing code? Write the numbers of adverbial clauses of time that consist of ...

- two words
- three words
- one word with three syllables

... and unlock the padlock!

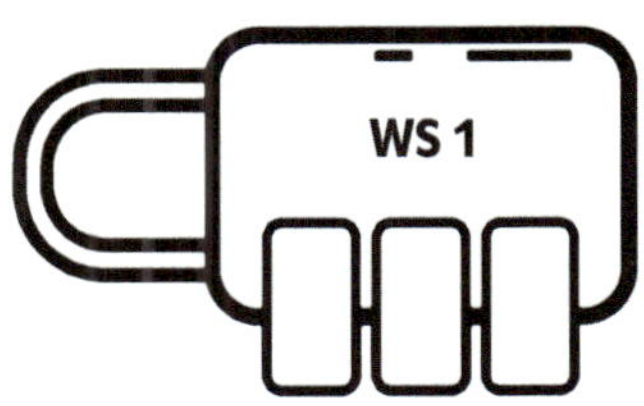

Edu Breakout Englisch – Escape Games für die 9./10. Klasse
ISBN 978-3-12-506685-4

Clues used ✓		
①	②	③

Can you complete the sentences?

Situation

Well done! You won the competition!

You and your classmates are the first visitors to enter the exhibition, and you all have VIP passes and bags of prizes. It's an amazing exhibition, and you're having a great day.

You enter the final room of the exhibition, and your teacher tells you there is another competition. This one is for pairs.

You and your partner each have halves of ten sentences. Firstly, can you complete your questions with words from the cards? Then work with your partner to match your sentences by reading them aloud. (Don't show each other your worksheets!)

cies | environ | mental

tion | natu

Sentence beginnings:

1 Before the industrial revolution, our planet was home to a rich diversity of .... ,

2 As soon as .... levels began to rise,

3 Once .... production became widespread,

4 By the time .... regulations were carried out,

5 Whenever deforestation and the loss of .... habitat occurs,

tic | plas

Sentence endings (for your partner):

A numerous species lose their homes and struggle to survive.
B animals have been forced to leave their habitats and migrate.
C some species face immediate threats and may even be lost.
D it may be too late to reverse some of the effects of our behaviour.
E the decline of endangered species will continue at an alarming rate.

spe | ral | pollu

What is the missing code? Write the numbers and unlock the padlock!

- the number of prepositions in completed sentence 1)
- the number of letters in the missing word in sentence 3)
- the number of verbs in completed sentence 5)

WS 2A

Edu Breakout Englisch – Escape Games für die 9./10. Klasse
ISBN 978-3-12-506685-4
Alles Digitale auf allango.net

Can you complete the sentences?

Clues used ✓		
①	②	③

Situation

Well done! You won the competition!

You and your classmates are the first visitors to enter the exhibition, and you all have VIP passes and bags of prizes. It's an amazing exhibition, and you're having a great day.

You enter the final room of the exhibition, and your teacher tells you there is another competition. This one is for pairs.

You and your partner each have halves of ten sentences. Firstly, can you complete your questions with words from the cards? Then work with your partner to match your sentences by reading them aloud. (Don't show each other your worksheets!)

cli | conser | da | vation | ex | treme | habi | tats | mate | mage

Sentence beginnings:

6 Since the onset of .... change,

7 Until stricter .... measures are established,

8 When .... are destroyed for urban development,

9 After .... weather events,

10 By the time we fully appreciate the .... caused by human activity,

Sentence endings (for your partner):

F we observed certain species starting to decline.
G it contributes to the loss of biodiversity and worsens the climate crisis.
H but many of these are now at risk due to habitat destruction.
I permanent damage had already been done to many of our ecosystems.
J marine ecosystems began to suffer from the plastic waste ending up in our waters.

What is the missing code? Write the numbers and unlock the padlock!

- the number of prepositions in completed sentence 6)
- the number of verbs in completed sentence 8)
- the number of letters in the missing word in sentence 10)

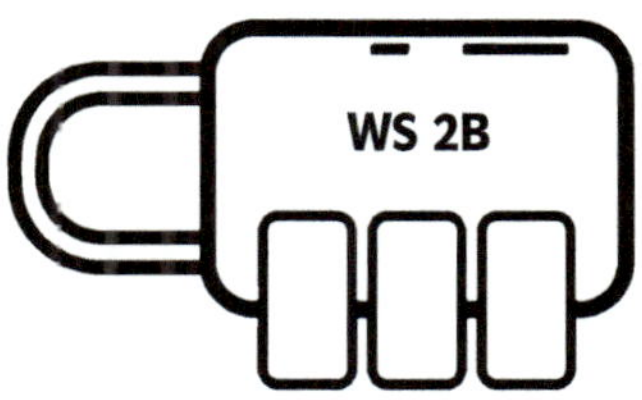

Treeboggle

Can you complete the poem?

Rationale
The students practise their reading and speaking skills to complete these puzzles. They also practise their basic writing skills.

Students practise and revise cleft sentences with *What* and *so/such* through the context of visiting a planet called Treeboggle.

Situation
In Worksheet 1, students solve a puzzle to complete a poem with so and such. In Worksheet 2, students put phrases in the correct order to make cleft sentences with *so* and *such*. In Worksheet 3, students find and correct grammatical errors in some reviews.

Differentiation
You can give groups who finish early, a related extension task. For example:
- Worksheet 1: Students continue the poem by writing (at least) another two lines for the poem.
- Worksheet 2: Students write (at least) another two cleft sentences about trees.
- Worksheet 3: Students write their own review using cleft sentences with *What* and *so/such*.

Solutions
Worksheet 1
1 such
2 so
3 such
4 so
5 so
6 such
7 so
8 so
9 such

Worksheet 2
1 What is so special about trees is that they provide a habitat for many animals.
2 What surprises me most about trees is how they survive in such challenging locations.
3 What I really like about trees is that there are so many different species.
4 What I find amazing about trees is that they grow from such tiny seeds.

Worksheet 3
Ben_B: What was astounding to me **was** that trees have got **such** a communication system – they talk to each other through their roots.
Tree-me: What makes trees **so** important to my planet is **that** they help clean the Earth's air by storing carbon.
Max15x: What upset me most is **finding** out that there has been **such** a lot of deforestation on Earth.
GreenGirl_123: What we need to remember about trees is that **we** need to give them **so** much protection and respect.

Language focus
- cleft sentences with *What* and *so/such*

Codes & clues

WS 1 5 4 9
Clue 1
Each of the two words begin with *s*.

Clue 2
We use so before an adjective, adverb, or quantifier.

Clue 3
We use *such* before a noun or an adjective + noun.

WS 2 1 1 0
Clue 1
Cleft sentences begin with *What* + subject or verb.

Clue 2
These cleft sentences have two clauses: the first begins with *What* and the other includes to *be* + *that/how*.

Clue 3
The second clause in these cleft sentences gives the explanation.

WS 3 2 1 5
Clue 1
The tense in the first clause must match the tense in the second clause.

Clue 2
The pronouns in the second clause must make sense with the pronouns in the first clause.

Clue 3
We use so before an adjective, adverb, or quantifier. We use *such* before a noun or an adjective + noun.

Clues used ✓		
①	②	③

Can you complete the poem?

Situation

You are in a spaceship travelling around the galaxy. You've visited a few planets already, and the space ship has just landed on another planet. The tour guide announces your arrival on 'Treeboggle': the planet of trees. The door opens, and you step outside into a forest. It's an unusual forest, because the trees appear to be moving and watching you. Then a small tree, wearing a **crown**, moves forward and **challenges** you to complete a poem.

to challenge *herausfordern*

Can you use the letters in the blue boxes to make two words ... and then complete the gaps in the poem with those two words?

On this planet, where trees stand proud and tall,

From (1) .... tiny seeds, most grew big
but some stayed small.

They move (2) .... gently in the breeze,

They're (3) .... peaceful giants, here to please.

Their leaves are green, like a big umbrella,With (4) .... many
shades, not like mozzarella!

They reach (5) .... high up to the sky,

It's (6) .... a sight, it makes me sigh.

With roots (7) .... deep, they stand (8) .... strong,

And are (9) .... safe homes, to birds with song.

What is the missing code? Write the numbers and unlock the padlock!

- the number of answers with two letters
- the number of answers with four letters
- the total number of vowels in all the answers

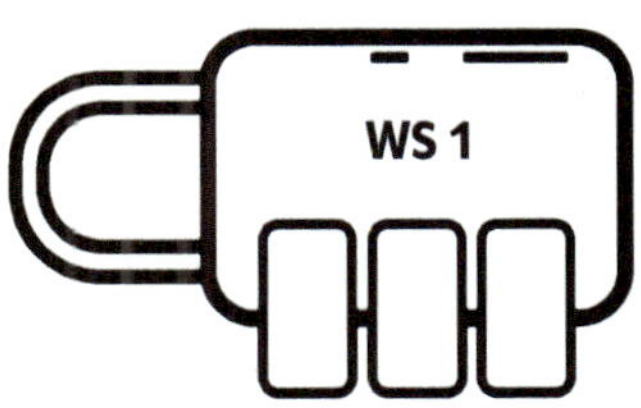

ISBN 978-3-12-506685-4

Clues used ✓		
①	②	③

Can you make sentences?

Situation

Well done! You solved the puzzle and completed the poem!

The king **bows** to you. A few trees start to move and then a small path opens between them. Your tour guide leads you down the path. She **announces**, "What I'll do now is let my friends tell you why I love trees." She points up to the trees and you see that there are lots of signs hanging from their branches.

to bow *herunterbeugen* • **to announce** *ankündigen*

Can you put the phrases in the correct order to make sentences?

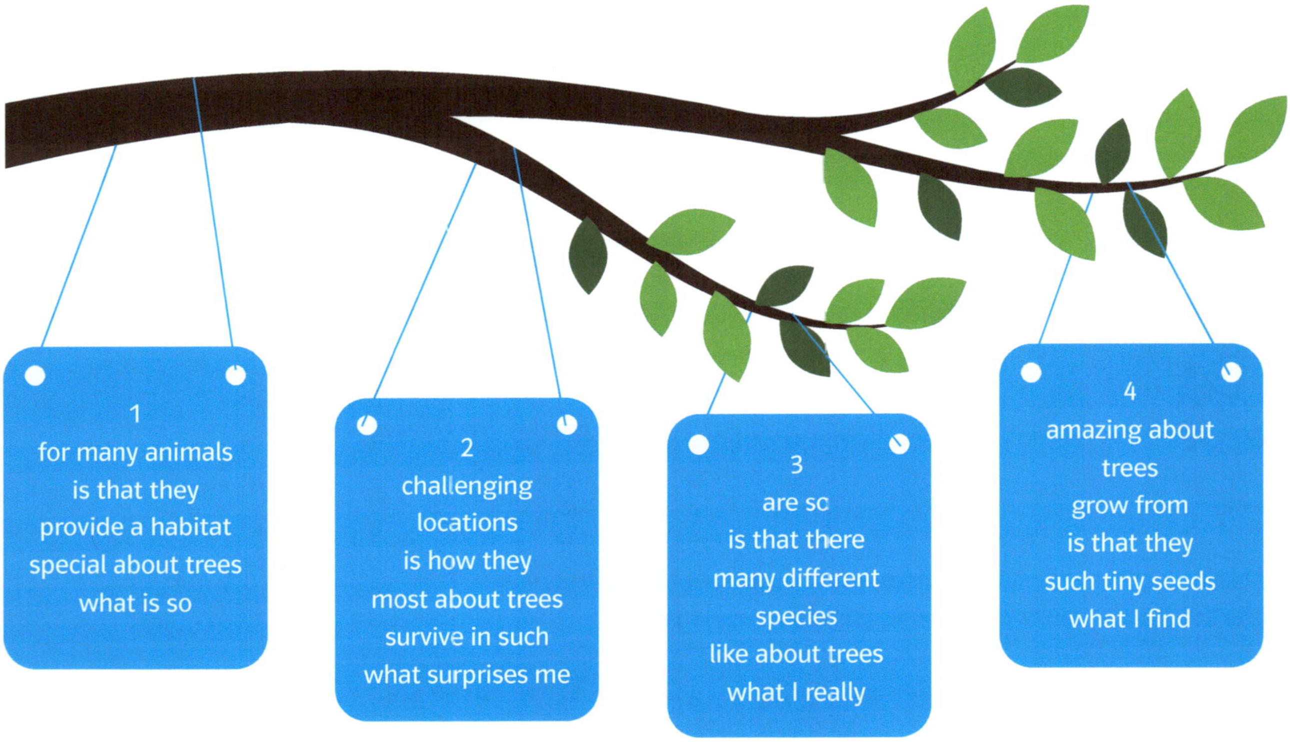

1 ....

2 ....

3 ....

4 ....

What is the missing code? Add the total number of letters in the fourth word of each sentence, and times that number by five. Then write the number and unlock the padlock!

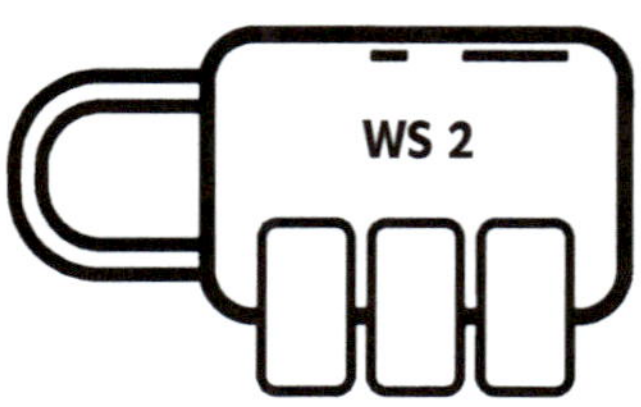

Edu Breakout Englisch – Escape Games für die 9./10. Klasse
ISBN 978-3-12-506685-4
Alles Digitale auf allango.net

Clues used ✓		
①	②	③

Can you find the errors?

Situation

Well done! You made the sentences!

You spend the day on the planet learning about trees. When it is time to leave, your tour guide asks you to leave a **review** on their website. She also asks if you can help correct the grammatical errors in some reviews from other tourists. If you can find and correct the errors, she will offer you a free trip back to Treeboggle.

review *Bewertung*

Can you find the eight errors in the reviews?

TREEBOGGLE: TOUR REVIEWS 1,768 ★★★★★

Ben_B ★★★★★
Amazing! What was astounding to me is that trees have got so a cool communication system – they talk to each other through their roots.

Tree-me ★★★★★
I love this planet! What makes trees such important to my planet is what they help clean the Earth's air by storing carbon.

Max15x ★★☆☆☆
The tour made me sad. What upset me most is find out that there has been so a lot of deforestation on Earth.

GreenGirl_123 ★★★★★
Really interesting! What we need to remember about trees is that they need to give them such much protection and respect.

What is the missing code? Write the numbers and unlock the padlock!

- the number of errors with verbs
- the number of errors with pronouns
- the number of other errors

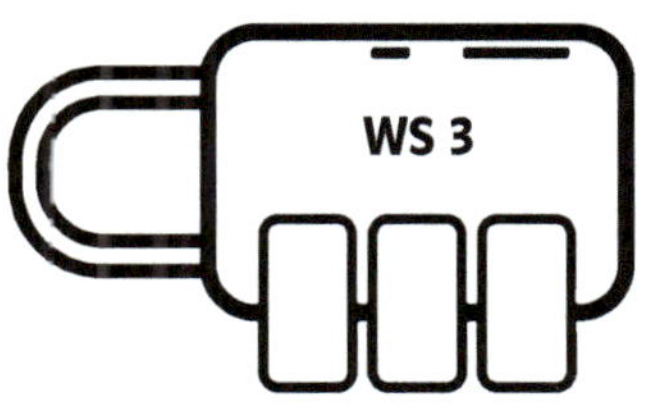

Edu Breakout Englisch – Escape Games für die 9./10. Klasse
ISBN 978-3-12-506685-4

Science fair

Can you complete the form?

Rationale
The students practise their reading and speaking skills to complete these puzzles. They also practise their basic writing skills.

Students practise and revise infinitive constructions through the context of a science fair and virtual reality.

Situation
In Worksheet 1, students identify a missing word and add it to the correct places in a form. In Worksheet 2, students solve a puzzle to complete instructions about using a virtual reality headset. In Worksheet 3, students put words together to make comments.

Differentiation
You can give groups who finish early, a related extension task. For example:
- Worksheet 1: Students complete the form with their own ideas for a science project.
- Worksheet 2: Students write another instruction for using headsets.
- Worksheet 3: Students write their own comment about the project using sentences with infinitive constructions (*to* + verb).

Solutions
Worksheet 1
1 this form **to** enter
2 Our goal is **to** share
3 **To** offer an amazing virtual reality experience
4 the group different tasks **to** complete
5 the best person **to** give the presentation is Ana,
6 **To** collaborate well, we must remember
7 a poster **to** show how
8 We want **to** win!

Worksheet 2
1 To use
2 to put
3 to make
4 to play
5 to navigate
6 to interact
7 To enjoy
8 concentrate
9 to explore
10 to take
11 to enter
12 to engage

Worksheet 3
1 I hope to learn more about virtual reality in the future.
2 I plan to ask my mum to buy me a headset.
3 To get a good job in virtual reality is my goal.
4 The aim of this project was to demonstrate how headsets work.
5 This group worked hard to present information about virtual reality.

Language focus
- infinitive constructions

Codes & clues

WS 1 **3 1 1**
Clue 1
The missing word has got two letters.

Clue 2
Look at the verbs. Are there any missing words before some of them?

Clue 3
Two of the missing words are the first word in a sentence.

WS 2 **5 3 5**
Clue 1
Start with the first letter in the top left corner of the puzzle.

Clue 2
Move from left to right, and continue to the row below.

Clue 3
The verbs in the puzzle are not in the same order as the gaps.

WS 3 **1 2 3**
Clue 1
To + infinitive can appear before the main clause of a sentence.

Clue 2
To + infinitive can introduce a goal or intention.

Clue 3
To + infinitive can give an explanation or a reason.

Clues used ✓		
①	②	③

Can you complete the form?

Situation

There is a science fair at your school next month. You and your friends are very excited about your project on virtual reality.

You teacher has given you a form to complete about your project. Your project leader has already completed the form, but they have missed one word … and they have missed the word eight times!

What is the missing word? Can you add this word to EIGHT places in the form?

ENTRY FORM FOR SCIENCE FAIR

You must complete this form enter your project in the science fair.

Project name: *We love virtual reality!*

What are the two main goals of your project?

1 *Our goal is share information about our favourite topic.*

2 *offer an amazing virtual reality experience for our classmates is our other goal.*

Describe two ways you will work together.

1 *Our project leader has given the group different tasks complete. For example, the best person give the presentation is Ana, because she is a confident speaker.*

2 *collaborate well, we must remember to listen carefully and take turns when speaking.*

What materials will you use?

We've made a poster show how the headset is operated.

Which room would you prefer at the fair: the main hall or room 4B?

We would rather be in the main hall.

Thank you! There is a prize for the project with the most votes!

Great! We want win. ☺

What is the missing code? Write the numbers and unlock the padlock!

- the lowest number of letters in the verb after the missing word
- the highest number of letters in the verb after the missing word

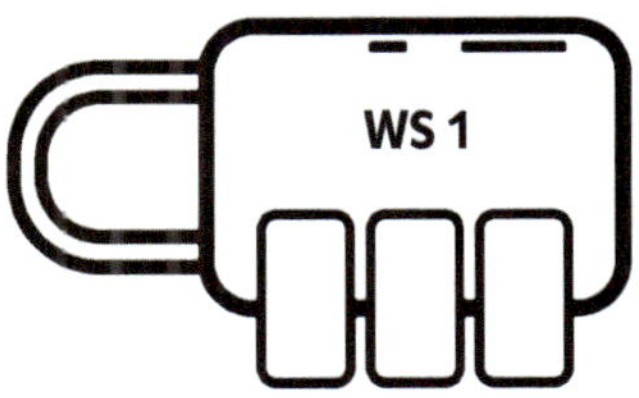

Edu Breakout Englisch –
Escape Games für die 9./10. Klasse
ISBN 978-3-12-506685-4

Clues used ✓		
①	②	③

Can you complete the instructions?

Situation

Well done! Your project has been entered for the science fair!

You and your group are now working on your project. Your group leader has made a puzzle for your classmates to solve *before* they can try the headset. She wants you to help her. Can you solve the puzzle?

Can you find the verbs and complete the instructions with the correct form of the verbs?

(1) __________ a VR headset, first, you need
(2) __________ it on your head. Adjust the straps
(3) __________ sure it fits comfortably.

Turn on the headset and select the game you want
(4) __________.

Pick up the controllers with your hands and use them
(5) __________ through the menu and
(6) __________ with objects in the virtual world.

(7) __________ the immersive experience fully,
(8) __________ on the visuals and sounds around you. Take your time
(9) __________ all of the different virtual worlds and scenarios.

Remember (10) __________ breaks if you start feeling dizzy or tired.

Overall, using a VR headset allows you
(11) __________ exciting new realms and
(12) __________ in immersive experiences like never before.

ENGA
GEEN
JOYC
ONCE
NTRA
TEIN
TERA
CTEX
PLOR
ENAV
IGAT
EPLA
YPUT
MAKE
ENTE
RTAK
EUSE

What is the missing code? Write the numbers and unlock the padlock!

- the number of vowels in the answer for number 5
- the number of syllables in the verb in number 6
- the number of consonants in the answer for number 9

WS 2

Edu Breakout Englisch – Escape Games für die 9./10. Klasse
ISBN 978-3-12-506685-4

Alles Digitale auf allango.net

Clues used ✓		
①	②	③

Can you complete the comments?

Situation

Well done! You helped your group leader!

The day of the fair is now here! Your project is very popular, and lots of your classmates listened to Ana's talk. You have asked your classmates to leave comments and to vote for you, because you want to win the prize.

However, there has been a problem and their comments have got **mixed up**.

to mix up *durcheinanderbringen*

Can you put the words together to complete the comments?

(1) Neat project!

....

....

about / future. / hope / I / in / reality / learn / more / the / to / virtual

(2) Headsets are cool!

....

....

a / ask / buy / headset. / I / me / mum / my / plan / to / to

(3) ....

....

I found this project very interesting.

a / get / goal. / good / in / is / job / my / To / virtual reality

about / group / hard / information / virtual / present / This / to / reality. / worked

(4) Very useful.

....

....

aim / demonstrate / headsets / how / of / project / The / this / to / was / work.

(5) ....

....

They did okay.

What is the missing code? Write the numbers and unlock the padlock!

The number of sentences where the missing word from worksheet 1 is …

- the first word in the sentence.
- the third word in the sentence.
- near the middle of the sentence.

WS 3

Edu Breakout Englisch – Escape Games für die 9./10. Klasse
ISBN 978-3-12-506685-4

Literary legends

Can you solve the code?

Rationale

The students practise their reading and speaking skills to complete these puzzles. They also practise their basic writing skills.

Students practise and revise adverbial clauses of result as well as basic spelling through the context of English literature.

Situation

In Worksheet 1, students solve a phonetic code to complete a message. In Worksheet 2, students use letters of the alphabet to complete English literature titles and author names. In Worksheet 3, students solve a riddle about a book.

Differentiation

You can give groups who finish early, a related extension task. For example:

- Worksheet 1: Students write their own name in phonetic code and/or choose three other words from the message and write the phonetic code.
- Worksheet 2: Students write the title and author of another English language book they know and write a sentence to describe it, using *so/such* if possible.
- Worksheet 3: Students write another two lines of the riddle or students write a new riddle/set of clues about another famous English language book or character from the book (they can choose titles from this escape game).

Solutions

Worksheet 1

1 carefully
2 importance
3 fortunate
4 amazing
5 characters

Worksheet 2

Q, V, X, Z

1 *Beowulf* by Anonymous
2 *The Canterbury Tales* by Geoffrey Chaucer
3 *Hamlet* by William Shakespeare
4 *Paradise Lost* by John Milton
5 *Frankenstein by* Mary Shelley
6 *The Great Gatsby* by F. Scott Fitzgerald
7 *Harry Potter and the philosopher's stone* by J.K. Rowling

Worksheet 3

1 so large
2 so silently
3 so dramatically
4 such strong friendships
5 such an incredible ring
6 such a big secret

THE LORD OF THE RINGS

Language focus

- adverbial clauses of result

Codes & clues

WS 1 1 1 5

Clue 1
There are three syllables in each gap.

Clue 2
Use an adjective or an adverb after *so*.

Clue 3
Use an adjective/quantifier + noun after *such*.

WS 2 6 1 7

Clue 1
The missing first letters of words in the titles are: *B, C, F, G, H, L, P*, and *T*.

Clue 2
The missing first letters in the authors' first names and family names are: *A, J, K, R, S*, and *W*.

Clue 3
The missing final letters in the authors' family names are: *D, E*, and *Y*

WS 3 3 1 2

Clue 1
Use words from both rings to complete the gaps.

Clue 2
Use *so* + adverb/adjective + *that* to make an adverbial clause of result.

Clue 3
Use *such* + adjective + plural noun + that or *such a/an* + countable noun + that to make an adverbial clause of result.

Can you solve the code?

Clues used ✓		
①	②	③

Situation

You are doing your homework in your bedroom. Your last piece of homework is to read one chapter of a new book. You take the book out of your backpack, but it looks different. There aren't any words on the pages or the cover. It's completely **blank**! "Where is my book?" you think. You **flick through** the pages again and suddenly lots of words start to appear …

blank *leer* • **to flick through** *durchblättern*

Can you solve the code for the missing words?

Now, read this so
(1) __________ (ˈkeəfəliː)
that you understand it all!
I'm not your average book;
oh no, not at all!

This message is of such great
(2) __________ (ɪmˈpɔːtəns)
that you must read it NOW!
Congratulations! You've got a
talking book! Take a bow!

You're so (3) __________
(ˈfɔːtʃənət) that I can play
games as well as tell stories.

I know such a lot of
(4) __________ (əˈmeɪzɪŋ)
tales that are full of glories.

There are so many
(5) __________ (ˈkærəktərs)
and places that I want to
share, but I'm not sure where
to begin; where, oh where?

Let's start with this code for you to try to break.

Be careful though – try not to make a mistake!

What is the missing code? Write the numbers and unlock the padlock!

- the number of answers with seven letters
- the number of adjectives + countable nouns following such
- the number of the last letter of answer 3 in the alphabet

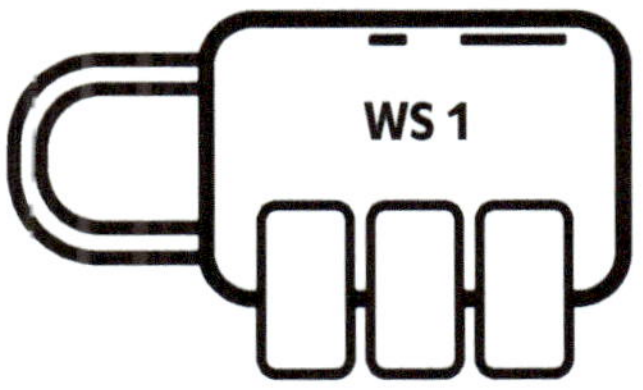

ISBN 978-3-12-506685-4

Clues used ✓		
①	②	③

Can you complete the titles and authors?

Situation

Well done! You solved the code!

More words begin to appear. There's a new puzzle.

Here are some of the stories I know. Do you know what they are?
Use each letter of the alphabet ONCE to complete the titles and authors.
Which four letters of the alphabet do you not need?

(1) _*eowulf* by _nonymous
This was made into a film with Angelina Jolie in 2007, but the original poem is so old that no one knows who the author is.

(2) _*he* _*anterbury Tales* by Geoffrey Cha_cer
This was written in the 14th century and the language is so different that many people find it difficult to understand.

(3) *Ha_let* by _illiam _hakespear_
There are such a lot of actors that want to be in this play about the Prince of Denmark and murder.

(4) *Paradise _ost* by John Milton
This is such a long poem that you may or may not finish reading it! It consists of ten books and was written in the 17th century.

(5) _*ranke_stein* by Mary Shelle_
This is such a scary tale that I had nightmares! It's about a scientist who creates a very famous monster.

(6) *The _reat Gatsby* by F. Scott Fitzgeral_
This American story has got such an interesting viewpoint on how money affects its characters. It's set in the Jazz Age and has a sad ending.

(7) _*arry* _*otter and the ph_losopher's st_ne* by _._. _owling
I read this book so quickly that my eyes hurt! It's the first of a series of very famous books and films.

What is the missing code? Write the numbers and unlock the padlock!

- the number of syllables in item 2's title
- the number of silent letters in item 4's title
- the total number of consonants in item 7's author

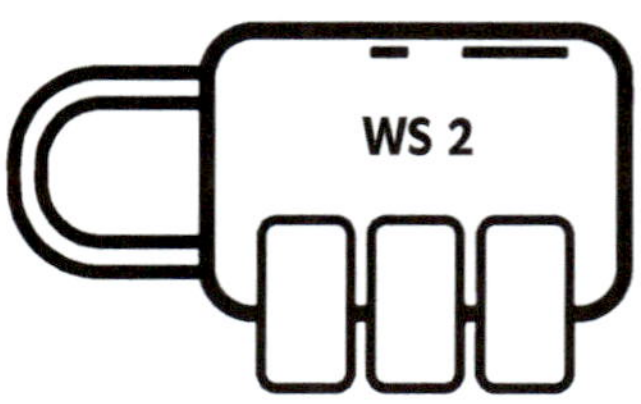

Edu Breakout Englisch – Escape Games für die 9./10. Klasse
ISBN 978-3-12-506685-4
Alles Digitale auf allango.net

Clues used ✓		
①	②	③

Can you solve the riddle?

Situation

Well done! You worked out the titles and their authors!

You close the book and look at the cover again. It's changed! Part of the title is now on the cover. You flick through the pages and there's the story! You can start your homework now. You try to go to the first chapter, but now the pages won't turn! More words begin to appear …

It's nearly time for your homework! But first, what are the missing words in my riddle and what is my title? Guess correctly, and I will open my pages for you.

THE _ _ _ _
OF THE
_ _ _ _S

large
big secret
dramatically
incredible ring
silently
strong friendship

such
so (x 3)
such an
such a

The world in this story is

(1) __________ that it is deeper

than the night, and its shadows

move (2) ____________ that

they scare the light.

This quest begins

(3) ____________ with our

heroes preparing for war.

They are stronger and braver

than anyone before.

There are tales of (4) ___________

that have already been told. But

this one is different – it's nothing

but gold.

The tale is about (5) ____________

that many want to wear, not just a

lord or a king.

But no other rings have got

(6) ____________ to share, that

they could change the world and

bring despair.

What is the missing code? Write the numbers and unlock the padlock!

- the number of answers with two words
- the number of answers with three words
- the number of answers with four words

WS 3

Edu Breakout Englisch –
Escape Games für die 9./10. Klasse
ISBN 978-3-12-506685-4

English explorer

Can you solve the riddle?

Rationale

The students practise their reading and speaking skills to complete these puzzles. They also practise their basic writing skills.

Students practise and revise participle constructions and infinitive constructions through the context of English-speaking countries.

Situation

In Worksheet 1, students solve a riddle about different English-speaking countries. In Worksheet 2, students sort a set of cards to make sentences about different food and countries. In Worksheet 3, students correct errors in their group's descriptions of food habits.

Differentiation

You can give groups who finish early, a related extension task. For example:

- Worksheet 1: Students write a short description of another country and its dish or food product.
- Worksheet 2: Students choose one completed sentence and add (at least) two more sentences to it.
- Worksheet 3: Students write their own description of their food habits.

Solutions

Worksheet 1

1 England; pudding, stuffing
2 Scotland; haggis
3 Wales; rarebit
4 Ireland; Irish, soda
5 Canada; Atlantic, butter, sugar
6 Australia; hemisphere, Vegemite,
7 New Zealand; Tasman, pokey, kiwi

Worksheet 3

1	to eat	6	correct
2	to go	7	making
3	correct	8	to teach
4	to have	9	correct
5	correct	10	Eating

Worksheet 2

stew = Eintopf; jerk chicken = Hähnchen auf jamaikanische Art (sehr würzig mariniert); gravy = Bratensoße

1 To indulge in … → **5** … have to try …
5 To fully experience … → **6** … eat roast turkey …
6 Eating spicy food … → **3** … is my favourite …
3 I like to … → **2** … prepare the vegetables …
2 Talking to my … → **8** … them I had …
8 My dream is … → **7** … have a barbecue …
7 I'm learning to … → **1** … thanks to YouTube …

Extra: card: **4**

Language focus

- participle constructions
- infinitive constructions

Codes & clues

WS 1 2 4 3

Clue 1
Match the number of letters in the final syllable with the number of write-on lines.

Clue 2
England is a country where people often eat roast dinners on Sundays.

Clue 3
The Southern Hemisphere includes many countries such as Australia, Brazil, Indonesia, and New Zealand.

WS 2 2 1 2

Clue 1
Read all the sentences and look for matching topics.

Clue 2
Try to match the name of the dish to the day or the country.

Clue 3
When you have sorted the cards, read through the completed sentence again and check if the grammar is correct.

WS 3 6 3 1

Clue 1
Emotion verbs (e.g., *love, hate*) can be followed by the infinitive or the gerund form of the verb.

Clue 2
The first word in a participle clause is the participle form of the verb.

Clue 3
Certain verbs are followed by a noun and the infinitive form of the main verb, e.g., *ask a question to someone.*

Clues used ✓		
①	②	③

Can you solve the riddle?

Situation

At school, your class is learning about different countries around the world. Your teacher sets you a riddle for homework.

Can you solve the riddle?

bit | da | dding | ffing | gar | ggis | key | man | mite | phere | sh | tic | tter | wi

(1) Starting in this country, I ate a roast dinner with Yorkshire pu_ _ _ _ _ and stu_ _ _ _ _.

(2) Travelling north to a country that borders the first one, I saw a dish called ha_ _ _ _. I didn't want to try this though!

(3) Travelling back south into the first country, and then going to another country that borders the first one, I tried Welsh rare_ _ _.

(4) Sailing across the Iri_ _ Sea to another country, I had some delicious so_ _ bread with my stew.

(5) Crossing the North Atlan_ _ _ Ocean and through the Labrador Sea, you might want to order a bu_ _ _ _ tart or a su_ _ _ pie.

(6) Flying down under and to the other side of the world and to the Southern Hemis_ _ _ _ _ , you should put Vege_ _ _ _ on your toast or eat a Tim Tam.

(7) Popping across the Tas_ _ _ Sea, you've got to try some hokey po_ _ _ ice cream or the healthier option – ki_ _ fruit.

Which countries have I been to? What are the dishes?

1 ....

2 ....

3 ....

4 ....

5 ....

6 ....

7 ....

What is the missing code? Write the numbers and unlock the padlock

- the number of silent e in the completed answers
- the number of countries in the United Kingdom
- the number of syllables in the longest completed answer

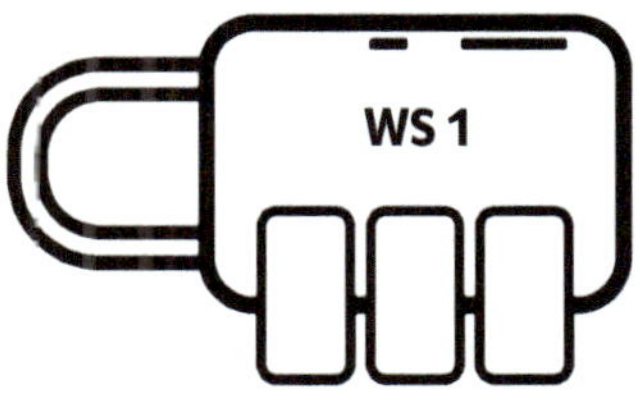

Edu Breakout Englisch – Escape Games für die 9./10. Klasse
ISBN 978-3-12-506685-4

Clues used ✓		
①	②	③

Can you sort the cards?

Situation

Well done! You solved the riddle!

Now your teacher asks for your help. She has made a game of cards with information about different countries. However, she has dropped them, and she needs to put them in the correct order.

Can you sort the cards? There is one extra card that you do not need.

Card	Top	Bottom
1	… thanks to YouTube videos by chefs in India.	To indulge in something unhealthy but tasty, you …
2	… prepare the vegetables for her traditional stew.	Talking to my friends about England, I told …
3	… is my favourite, so I'd love to go to Jamaica.	I like to help my Irish grand-mother …
4	… cook for about four hours before you serve it.	Making steak pie is something I would …
5	… have to try poutine – French fries with cheese and a brown gravy.	To fully experience Thanksgiving Day, you should …
6	… eat roast turkey and then have a slice of pumpkin pie!	Eating spicy food like jerk chicken …
7	… have a barbecue with friends on the beach.	I'm learning to make butter chicken curry …
8	… them I had fish and chips there.	My dream is to work in Australia and …

What is the missing code? Write the numbers and unlock the padlock

- the number of correct sentences with a participle clause
- the number of correct sentences where the infinitive is a subject complement after a form of *be*
- the number of correct sentences where the infinitive is a subject

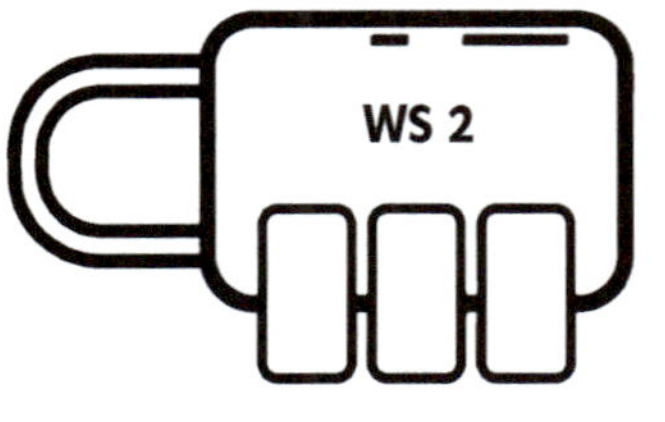

Edu Breakout Englisch – Escape Games für die 9./10. Klasse
ISBN 978-3-12-506685-4

Alles Digitale auf allango.net

Clues used ✓		
①	②	③

Can you correct the verbs?

Situation

Well done! You sorted the cards!

Your teacher gives the class another task: write about your food habits. Your group of three completes the task quickly. You all like doing partner feedback, so you swap your work. You read the others' work and notice some errors.

Are the ten verbs in bold type correct? If not, can you correct them for your partners?

I tend (1) **eat** toast for breakfast on school days. I put Vegemite on it. It's a dark, salty spread – you love it or hate it! I eat it quickly and then I'm ready (2) **going**! It's different at weekends. (3) **Eating** a big breakfast together on Sundays has become a tradition in my family. My sister always wants (4) **having** Welsh rarebit. It's a type of cheese sauce with lots of different spices on toast. Her dream is (5) **to run** her own café.

My goal this year is (6) **to learn** cookery skills. It's an essential life skill. I have already practised (7) **to make** pastries, like samosa. These are triangular and stuffed with vegetables or meat. I asked my grandmother (8) **teach** me some other traditional recipes. Now I know how (9) **to prepare** my favourite dessert – Gulab Jamun. It's made with milk, flour, syrup, spices, and rose water. (10) **Eat** it cold is what I prefer, but some people like it hot.

What is the missing code? Write the numbers and unlock the padlock

- the number of incorrect verbs
- the number of correct verbs in the infinitive form
- the number of correct verbs in the gerund form

WS 3

Edu Breakout Englisch – Escape Games für die 9./10. Klasse
ISBN 978-3-12-506685-4

The champions

Can you guess the sports?

Rationale

The students practise their reading and speaking skills to complete these puzzles. They also practise their basic writing skills.

Students practise and revise defining relative clauses and non-defining relative clauses through the context of spectating at a sports competition.

Situation

In Worksheet 1, students solve a code to identify three sports. In Worksheet 2, students complete a 'to do' list about volleyball. In Worksheet 3, students solve a puzzle to complete a description of an incident at the sports stadium.

Differentiation

You can give groups who finish early, a related extension task. For example:

- Worksheet 1: Students choose another sport and write a short description about it.
- Worksheet 2: Students write a short 'to do' list explaining how to prepare for playing a sport or game of their choice.
- Worksheet 3: Students write sentences about a sport competition using non-defining relative clauses.

Solutions

Worksheet 1

1 wheelchairs
2 strength
3 seated
4 ball
5 fighters
6 kicks
A wheelchair rugby
B sitting volleyball
C Tae kwon do

Worksheet 2

1 court
2 which
3 long
4 antennas
5 which
6 side
7 referees
8 whose
9 net
10 where
11 players
12 beyond
13 spectators
14 when
15 seats
16 players
17 who

Worksheet 3

1 when the champions
2 which shone
3 in which the trophies
4 where photos
5 where distinguished guests
6 through which spectators
7 who had won
HE SAID SORRY

Language focus

- defining relative clauses
- non-defining relative clauses

Codes & clues

WS 1 3 3 3
Clue 1
Each symbol represents a sound (or a 'phoneme').

Clue 2
The symbols for consonant sounds are very similar to the letters they represent.

Clue 3
One symbol may represent more than one letter.

WS 2 6 8 2
Clue 1
We use relative pronouns at the start of the non-defining relative clause.

Clue 2
We use *where* to talk about a location.
We use *when* to talk about time in some way.

Clue 3
We use *who* and *whose* to talk about people and possession. We use *which* to talk about things.

WS 3 2 1 5
Clue 1
The middle letter of each line spells a phrase.

Clue 2
The lines contain words without any spaces and which run on to the lines below.

Clue 3
The words make phrases which complete the gaps.

Clues used ✓		
①	②	③

Can you guess the sports?

Situation

You are a big fan of sports and today is your birthday. Your parents have given you some tickets for an international sports competition. You will be able to see three sports there. They haven't told you what the sports are, but they have written some clues for you on the envelope that contains your tickets.

Can you work out the words (1–6)? Can you guess the three sports (A–C)?

In a sport where players use (1) ________________ /ˈwiːltʃeəs/,
Where speed and (2) ________________ /streŋθ/ are key affairs,
(A) ________________ ________________, a game of respect,
The ball behind the line makes the goal correct.

Another game, (B) ________________ ________________'s the name,
Played by (3) ________________ /ˈsiːtɪd/ players, it's nearly the same,
With teamwork and (4) ________________ /bɔːl/ skills on display,
The ball mustn't touch the ground, the players may.

Lastly, in a ring where (5) ________________ /ˈfaɪtəs/ stand tall,
(C) ________________, this sport's admired by all, With
(6) ________________ /kɪks/ and punches, it's quite a sight,
Yet respect remains, both day and night.

	1	2	3	4	5
1	A	B	W	D	E
2	U	G	H	I	Y
3	L	M	Q	O	P
4	N	R	S	T	F
5	V	C	X	K	Z

A 13-23-15-15-31-52-23-11-24-42 42-21-22-12-25

B 43-24-44-44-24-41-22 51-34-31-31-15-25-12-11-31-31

C 44-11-15 54-13-34-41 14-34

What is the missing code? Write the numbers and unlock the padlock!

- the number of answers with one syllable
- the number of answers with a silent *h*
- the number of syllables in answer C

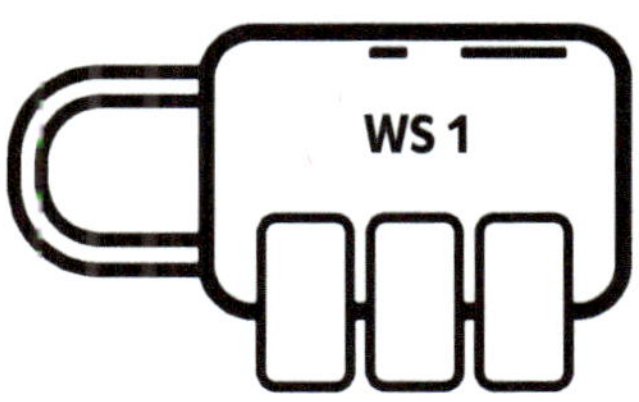

Edu Breakout Englisch –
Escape Games für die 9./10. Klasse
ISBN 978-3-12-506685-4

Clues used ✓		
①	②	③

Can you complete the list?

Situation

Well done! You worked out the words and correctly guessed the sports!

You have arrived at the sports stadium and are on a stadium tour. You're now at the volleyball courts. This is your favourite sport. You hear two stadium **staff** arguing nearby, and your parents ask them what is happening. The officials have an incomplete to-do list from their colleague, and they urgently need to prepare the courts, but they aren't experts in volleyball. Your parents smile and, pointing to you, say "There's your expert!"

staff *Personal*

Can you complete the 'to do' list for the officials? What extra words do you need?

antennas   beyond   court   long   net   players   players   referees   seats   side   spectators

Use a measuring tape to mark out the (1) ________ dimensions, (2) ________ should be 18 meters (3) ________ and 9 meters wide, and ensure these measurements are accurate.

Set up the (4) ________, (5) ________ are thin vertical rods, on each (6) ________ of the net.

The (7) ________, (8) ________ job is to ensure the rules are followed, will be positioned by the (9) ________ .

Team benches, (10) ________ the substitution (11) ________ will be sitting, need to be situated (12) ________ the sidelines of the court.

The (13) ________, (14) ________ entering the area, should be told to go to their (15) ________ and not walk on the courts.

It'll be a great match! The (16) ________, (17) ________ are trying for a place in the finals, will be playing their best.

What is the missing code? Write the numbers and unlock the padlock!

- the number of letters in the noun form of the answer to 3
- the number of letters in the verb form of the answer to 13
- the number of consonants in the singular form of the answer to number 15

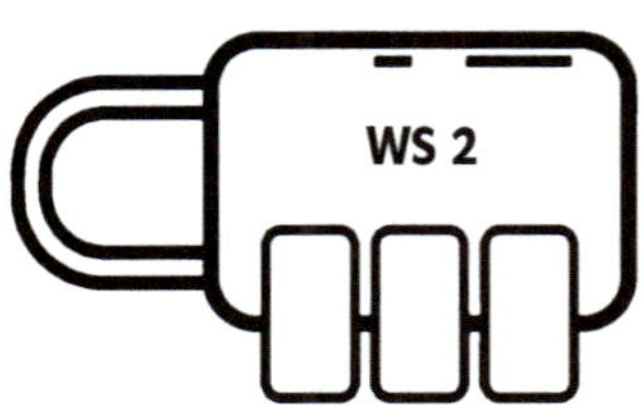

Edu Breakout Englisch – Escape Games für die 9./10. Klasse
ISBN 978-3-12-506685-4

Alles Digitale auf allango.net

Can you solve the code?

Clues used ✓		
①	②	③

Situation

Well done! You completed the 'to do' list!

You are now on the way home after an amazing day. You are looking through photos from the day on your mum's mobile phone when a news report flashes on the screen. There has been an **incident** at the stadium! In order to **access** the report, you need to solve a code.

incident *Vorfall* • **to access** *zugreifen auf*

Can you solve the code?

INWHIHCHTHE
TROPHEIESTH
ROUGHSWHICH
SPECTAATORS
~~WHENTIHECHA~~
~~MPIONDS~~WHER
EDISTSINGUI
SHEDGOUESTS
WHERERPHOTO
SWHICRHSHON
EWHOHYADWON

ATTEMPTED THEFT AT STADIUM

On the podium, (1) *when the champions* receive their prizes, someone would have presented the trophy to the winners. But the trophy had been stolen moments before.

The trophy, (2) ______________ ______________ beautifully, was last seen in the trophy room. This room, (3) ______________ are stored, is located on the top floor. The wall of fame, (4) ______________ ______________ of past champions holding the trophy can be seen, is on the same floor.

In the VIP lounge, (5) ______________ ______________ socialise, some people thought they saw a man running down the corridor. Near the entrance, (6) ______________ ______________ come in, sports lovers heard a loud alarm. A man was running fast and he was carrying the trophy.

He managed to get outside the building and was sprinting towards the stadium gates. He glanced up at the statue of the country's most legendary player, (7) ______________ ______________ the same trophy he was now holding countless times, and he stopped, and he said …

What did he say?

....

What is the missing code? Write the numbers and unlock the padlock!

- the number of answers with a preposition before the relative pronoun
- the number of answers in the past perfect
- the number of answers with countable nouns

WS 3

Alles Digitale auf allango.net

Edu Breakout Englisch – Escape Games für die 9./10. Klasse
ISBN 978-3-12-506685-4

Gaming

Can you complete the questions?

Rationale

The students practise their reading and speaking skills to complete these puzzles. They also practise their basic writing skills.

Students practise and revise future forms through the context of gaming.

Situation

In Worksheet 1, students use clues to solve a crossword about gaming. In Worksheet 2, students listen and solve a code to complete some answers. In Worksheet 3, students find four sentences in a maze.

Differentiation

You can give groups who finish early, a related extension task. For example:

- Worksheet 1: Students think of three more words related to gaming (or another free-time interest) and write definitions or clues for the three words. Then students swap with a partner and try to guess the words.
- Worksheet 2: Students write their own answers to the questions and/or write another question using a future form.
- Worksheet 3: Students write sentences describing what they will have done by next weekend and what they will be doing this time next Saturday.

Solutions

Worksheet 1

1	transform	A	will have transformed
2	enter	B	will shape
3	shape	C	will have lost
4	replace	D	will replace
5	lose	E	will have entered

Worksheet 2

won't	C – 1 won't maintain – 2 will have been invented – 3 will be
future simple	A – 4 will continue – 5 will change
future perfect passive	E – 6 will enter – 7 won't be expecting
future perfect	B – 8 will have revolutionised
future continuous	D – 9 will have witnessed – 10 will have been developed

Worksheet 3

- Tomorrow evening, our gaming club will be hosting a tournament where players will be competing for prizes.
- He won't reach the next level.
- By lunchtime, we'll have completed all the levels.
- This time next weekend, we'll be travelling to the e-sports tournament

Language focus

- future forms with *will*

Codes & clues

WS 1 3 1 3

Clue 1
The verbs in the crossword begin with *T, E, S, R,* and *L.*

Clue 2
We use the simple future (*will* + infinitive) for predictions about the future.

Clue 3
We use the future perfect (*will* + *have* + past participle) for actions that will have been completed by a specific time in the future.

WS 2 5 4 2

Clue 1
We form the simple future with *will*/*won't* + infinitive. We form the future continuous with *will* + *be* + *-ing.*

Clue 2
We form the future perfect with *will* + *have* + past participle.

Clue 3
We form the future perfect passive with *will* + *have* + *been* + past participle.

WS 3 3 1 1

Clue 1
Use the capital letters and punctuation to help you find the sentences.

Clue 2
Start in the top left corner and move clockwise … and continue.

Clue 3
The sentences are in a consecutive line of boxes.

Clues used ✓		
①	②	③

Can you complete the questions?

Situation

You are gaming online with your friends. Today, you're playing very well. In fact, you could be at the top of the **leaderboard**. You've nearly reached the next level when the screen goes black! A loud voice says, "So, you think you're good at gaming? Let's see how much you know!" Then a crossword appears on the screen along with a stopwatch set at two minutes. The stopwatch starts to count down …

leaderboard *Bestenliste*

Can you complete the questions with the correct future form of *will*?

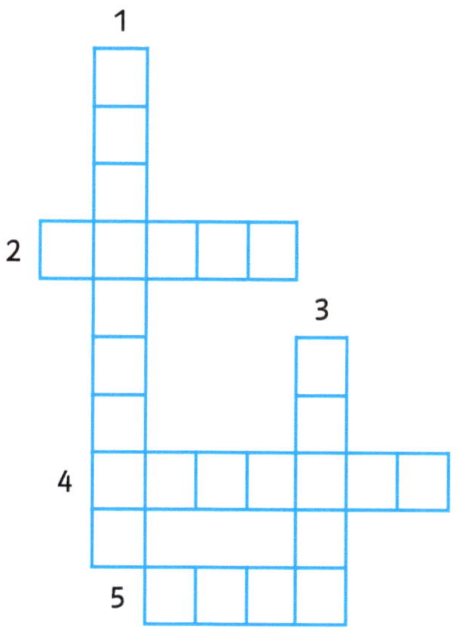

1 to completely change something and improve it

2 to go into or be included in something

3 to influence the development of something

4 to take the place of something or someone

5 to stop being popular or having success

A By 2030, do you think artificial intelligence ____________________ the gaming industry?

B Do you think augmented reality games ____________________ the future of outdoor entertainment?

C Within the next few years, do you think virtual reality headsets ____________________ their popularity?

D Do you think holographic gaming ____________________ traditional console gaming by 2040?

E By next summer, do you think virtual reality games ____________________ the mainstream entertainment?

What is the missing code? Write the numbers and unlock the padlock!

- the number of infinitive verb forms with two syllables
- the number of infinitive verb forms with stress on the first syllable
- the number of auxiliary verbs in the gaps in the questions

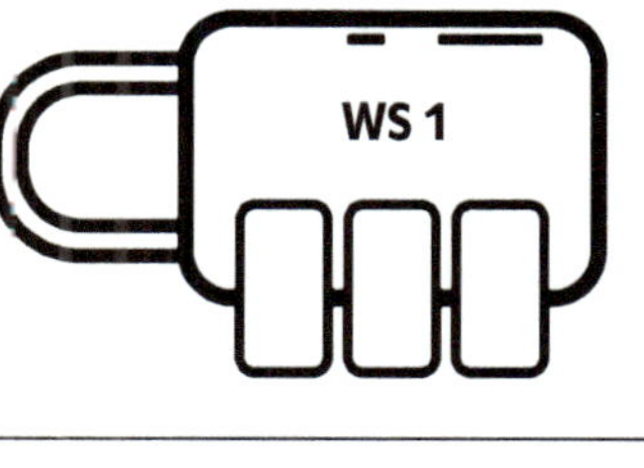

Edu Breakout Englisch – Escape Games für die 9./10. Klasse
ISBN 978-3-12-506685-4

Can you solve the code?

Clues used ✓		
①	②	③

Situation

Well done! You completed the crossword and the questions!

The voice speaks again. "Well played! Let's see if you can solve this code."

Can you solve the code and complete the answers? Then listen and match the questions to the answers.

	will	....	**future perfect passive**
....	***won't***	....	**future perfect**
....	**future simple**	....	**future continuous**

...... Yes, I think so. They (1) ________________ (maintain) their popularity. Perhaps something similar (2) ________________ (invent) in the next ten years, but it (3) ________________ (be) smaller and better ... and cheaper.

...... Yes and no. AI is already impacting the gaming industry! So, I think it (4) ________________ ________________ (continue) to play an ongoing role in the development of gaming rather than be a separate force that (5) ________________ (change) it.

...... No! I don't think they (6) ________________ (enter) mainstream entertainment at any point. I think we need different types of entertainment for different types of people and for different ages. But I (7) ________________ (expect) virtual reality games to be something I'd play with older members of my family, for example.

...... Definitely! It is the future! We're already using augmented reality in filters on social media. Within the next decade, augmented reality (8) ________________ (revolutionise) home entertainment – outdoors and indoors.

...... Maybe. It's difficult to say. By the time 2040 arrives, we (9) ________________ (witness) incredible advancements, so maybe other types of gaming (10) ________________ (develop) by then.

What is the missing code? Write the numbers and unlock the padlock!

- the number of syllables in the longest past participle answer
- the number of *have* auxiliary verbs in the answers
- the number of verb forms in the answers with only one syllable

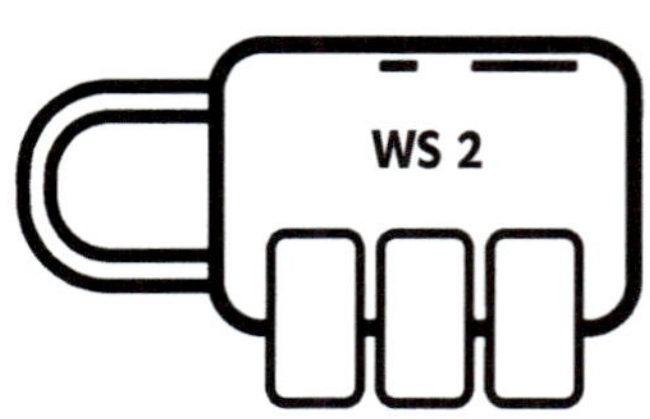

Edu Breakout Englisch – Escape Games für die 9./10. Klasse
ISBN 978-3-12-506685-4
Alles Digitale auf allango.net

Clues used ✓		
①	②	③

Can you find the sentences?

Situation

Well done! You solved the code!

The voice speaks again. "Well played – again! If you can find the four sentences in this maze, then your name will be at the top of the leaderboard … and you will have become the champion!"

Can you find four future sentences?

Tomorrow	players	evening,	will	our	be
next	have	This	level.	completed	gaming
where	we'll	be	travelling	time	competing
the	levels.	tournament.	to	By	club
tournament	we'll	e-sports	the	all	for
reach	weekend,	the	lunchtime,	next	will
a	won't	hosting	He	be	prizes.

What is the missing code? Write the numbers and unlock the padlock!

- the number of sentences with the future continuous
- the number of sentences with the future perfect
- the number of sentences with the future simple

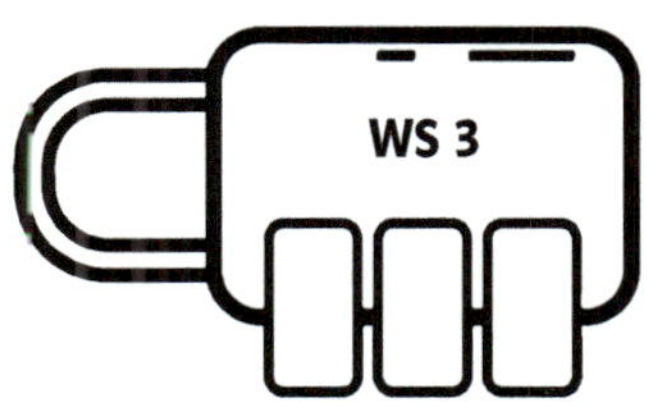

ISBN 978-3-12-506685-4

Beyond school 1

Can you complete the advice?

Rationale

The students practise their reading and speaking skills to complete these puzzles. They also practise their basic writing skills.

Students practise and revise modals through the context of preparing a blog for the school website.

Situation

In EG19–20, students learn about young adulthood. In Worksheet 1, students solve a code to complete advice about how to write a blog. In Worksheet 2A and 2B, students solve another code and work together to share advice for young adults.

Differentiation

You can give groups who finish early, a related extension task. For example:

- Worksheet 1: Students add more advice, using modal verbs.
- Worksheet 2A and 2B: Students write more pieces of advice for young adults, using modal verbs. Students could even write a short blog post on the topic.

Solutions

Worksheet 1

1. should brainstorm
2. might want
3. could collaborate
4. should create
5. could invest
6. should save
7. might wish
8. should check

Worksheet 2A

1-C ought, life
2-F need, responsibility
3-B might, independence
4 D could, mentors
5 E should, confidence
6-G might, hobbies
7-A could, goals

Worksheet 2B

1-F ought, mistakes
2-C need, confidence
3-A might, voluntary
4-E could, journals
5-G should, comfort
6-B might, cultures
7-D could, goals

Language focus

- modals

Codes & clues

WS 1 3 6 7
Clue 1
'X YILD' is a code for the words 'A BLOG'. If A equals X and B equals Y, … what is the code?

Clue 2
One of the missing modal verbs is a strong recommendation or suggestion.

Clue 3
One of the missing modal verbs is a possibility, but it is not certain. One of the others is a stronger possibility, but not compulsory.

WS 2A 3 4 1
Clue 1
'LFI YOLT' is a code for the words 'OUR BLOG'. If A equals Z, B equals Y, and C equals X, what is the code?

Clue 2
One of the missing modal verbs is a strong recommendation or suggestion. One of the others is a very strong recommendation or a necessity.

Clue 3
One of the missing modal verbs is a possibility, but it is not certain. One of the other is a stronger possibility, but not compulsory.

WS 2B 5 3 4
Clue 1
'LFI YOLT' is a code for the words 'OUR BLOG'. If A equals Z and B equals Y, … what is the code?

Clue 2
One of the missing modal verbs is a strong recommendation or suggestion. One of the others is a very strong recommendation or a necessity.

Clue 3
One of the missing modal verbs is a possibility, but it is not certain. One of the other is a stronger possibility, but not compulsory.

Can you complete the advice?

Clues used ✓		
①	②	③

Situation

You have just joined a new club at your school. The club looks after the school's website and social media accounts. They have asked you to write this week's blog, and you are very excited. They send you some **guidance**, but it's in a code. The club always use a code to protect their ideas from others.

guidance *Anleitung*

Can you complete the advice with the correct modal verbs?

ALPHA	a	b	c	d	e	f	g	h	i	j	k	l	m	n	o	p	q	r	s	t	u	v	w	x	y	z
CIPHER	x	y	z	a	b	c	d	e	f	g	h	i	j	k	l	m	n	o	p	q	r	s	t	u	v	w

1 You *PELRIA YOXFKPQLOJ* .... topics that are relevant and fun.

2 You *JFDEQ TXKQ* .... to explore different writing styles and find your 'voice'.

3 You *ZLRIA ZLIIXYLOXQB* .... with other bloggers and even write something together.

4 You *PELRIA ZOBXQB* .... **eye-catching** visuals to encourage readers to read your blog.

5 You *ZLRIA FKSBPQ* .... some time in learning about basic SEO principles but it's not essential.

6 You *PELRIA PXSB* .... your notes and drafts, so that you don't lose any important thoughts.

7 You *JFDEQ TFPE* .... to interact with comments made by your readers, because blogging is sometimes like a conversation.

8 You *PELRIA ZEBZH* .... and **proofread** your posts before you publish them.

eye-catching *ins Auge fallen* • **proofread** *Korrektur lesen*

What is the missing code? Write the numbers and unlock the padlock!

- the sentence number that refers to the possibility of writing with other people
- the sentence number that recommends protecting the development of your ideas
- the sentence number that suggests answering comments on your blog

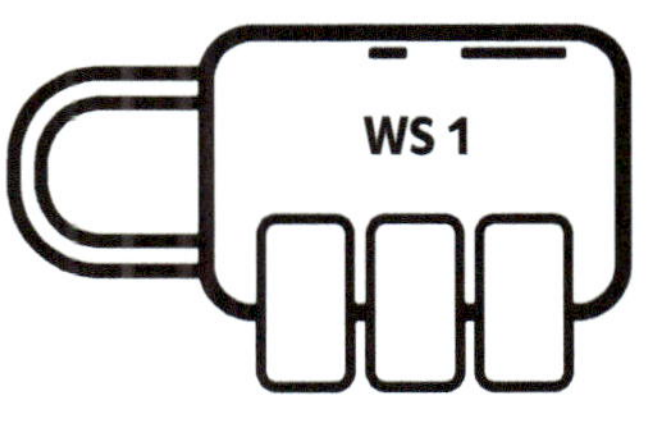

Edu Breakout Englisch – Escape Games für die 9./10. Klasse
ISBN 978-3-12-506685-4

Clues used ✓		
①	②	③

Can you solve the code?

Situation

Well done! You completed the advice!

You have chosen to write a blog about advice for young adults. You will collaborate with another writer, as the advice suggested. You and your friend have both done your research and made some notes. Now you're going to compare ideas and choose the best ones. There is a problem – you used a new code for your notes and you've forgotten it! The deadline is today, so you need to work out the code quickly!

You and your partner have similar notes. (Do not show each other your worksheets!) Can you solve the code? Then can you take turns to tell each other your advice and choose your favourite seven ideas?

MY NOTES FOR 'LFI YOLT' ('OUR BLOG')

A XLFOW, TLZOH
B NRTSG, RMWVKVMWVMXV
C LFTSG, ORUV
D XLFOW, NVMGLIH
E HSLFOW, XLMURWVMXV
F MVVW, IVHKLMHRYRORGB
G NRTSG, SLYYRVH

1 You .... to learn basic .... skills like cooking and grocery shopping .... because you can't exist on home deliveries forever.

2 You .... to develop a sense of .... by doing tasks without someone telling you to do them. Your future self will be happy that you regularly clean your bathroom.

3 You .... want to find a part-time job. Not only does it give you some financial ...., but perhaps you get to wear a cool uniform too!

4 You .... look for .... who inspire you and ask for their advice. Then you have to take the advice …

5 You .... practise saying „no" when necessary. This skill will save you from doing something you don't want to and you'll grow in .... Win win!

6 You .... consider exploring different .... and interests to work out what makes you truly happy. (And what you absolutely hate, too!)

7 You .... start setting .... for yourself, both short-term and long-term. Use a mood board of pictures or write a step-by-step plan to achieve your goals.

What is the missing code? Write the numbers and unlock the padlock!

- the sentence number that mentions money and clothes
- the sentence number that mentions a type of role model
- the sentence number that mentions food

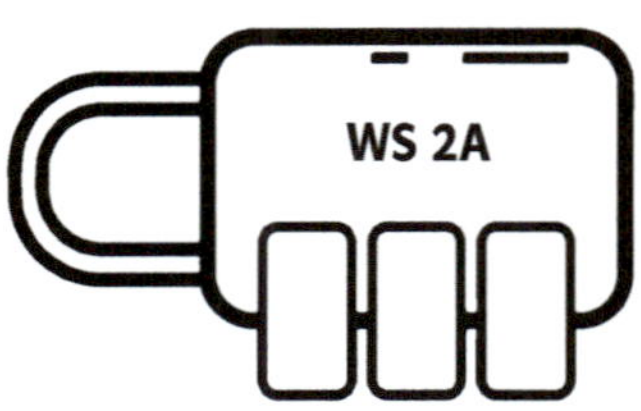

Edu Breakout Englisch – Escape Games für die 9./10. Klasse
ISBN 978-3-12-506685-4
Alles Digitale auf allango.net

Can you solve the code?

Clues used ✓		
①	②	③

Situation

Well done! You completed the advice!

You have chosen to write a blog about advice for young adults. You will collaborate with another writer, as the advice suggested. You and your friend have both done your research and made some notes. Now you're going to compare ideas and choose the best ones. There is a problem – you used a new code for your notes and you've forgotten it! The deadline is today, so you need to work out the code quickly!

You and your partner have similar notes. (Do not show each other your worksheets!) Can you solve the code? Then can you take turns to tell each other your advice and choose your favourite seven ideas?

MY NOTES FOR 'LFI YOLT' ('OUR BLOG')

A NRTSG, ELOFMGZIB
B NRTSG, XFOGFIVH
C MVVW, XLMURWVMXV
D XLFOW, TLZOH
E XLFOW, QLFIMZOH
F LFTSG, NRHGZPVH
G HSLFOW, XLNULIG

1 You .... to learn from your .... because you're going to make lots of them (and that's part of life's journey!).

2 You .... try to develop your ....and self-belief. Your future self will be very proud of you!

3 You .... want to do some ...., work. Not only does it give you some experience of the world of work, but you are giving help to others. Win win!

4 You .... look for apps that offer well-being activities, such as reflective .... But don't just download them, use them.

5 You .... practise saying "yes" to things that are slightly* outside of your .... zone. (*That doesn't include agreeing to go swimming with sharks.)

6 You ....consider exploring other countries by traveling and respectfully observing the .... of other people.

7 You .... start setting .... with your friends, perhaps you all want to go on a trip or build an app. Make plans together and enjoy the advantages of shared ideas.

What is the missing code? Write the numbers and unlock the padlock!

- the sentence number that mentions animals
- the sentence number that mentions a job without pay
- the sentence number that mentions digital behaviour

WS 2B

Edu Breakout Englisch – Escape Games für die 9./10. Klasse
ISBN 978-3-12-506685-4

Beyond school 2

Can you work out the topics?

Rationale

The students practise their reading and speaking skills to complete these puzzles. They also practise their basic writing skills.

Students practise and revise *wish* and *if only* through the context of preparing a blog for the school website.

Situation

In EG19–20, students learn about young adulthood. In Worksheet 1, students solve a code about topics related to young adulthood. In Worksheet 2, students choose the correct words to complete reviews of an app. In Worksheet 3, students complete an example message.

Differentiation

You can give groups who finish early, a related extension task. For example:

- Worksheet 1: Students make a list of other topics (alphabetically, if possible) that they would like to learn about.
- Worksheet 2: Students write a review (positive or negative) of an app they use.
- Worksheet 3: Students write their own message to their past teenage self, imagining they are already an adult.

Solutions

Worksheet 1

1 ambition
2 budgeting
3 communication
4 domestic
5 exercise
6 food

Worksheet 2

A 2 didn't have
B 6 would
C 7 I'd known
D 11 had listened
E 14 I had got
F 18 I'd done
G 19 were higher
H 23 only I'd

Worksheet 3

1 only
2 share
3 only
4 see
5 wish
6 'd/had known
7 only
8 be
9 wish
10 say
11 wish
12 'd/had enjoyed

Language focus

- *wish, if only*

Codes & clues

WS 1 3 6 2

Clue 1
Each item is one word divided into groups of two characters.

Clue 2
The first letter of each word has been replaced by the letter *x*.

Clue 3
An exclamation mark *(!)* indicates a new syllable.

WS 2 1 0 0

Clue 1
Use the present tense for comments about a current situation.

Clue 2
Use the past perfect for past events that happened before another event in the past.

Clue 3
Use a modal verb for hypothetical or unreal situations.

WS 3 2 3 3

Clue 1
Use pronoun + *wish* or *If only* + pronoun to express hopes and regrets.

Clue 2
Use the correct tense (e.g. present simple or past perfect) for the situation.

Clue 3
Use the infinitive form of a verb after a modal verb.

Can you name the cities?

Clues used ✓		
①	②	③

Situation

You and your friend recently wrote a blog for the school website and it was very popular! You have been asked to write another blog. They have asked you to write a blog about an app that helps teenagers.

You start searching online when an advert for an app pops up. However, some of the words have not displayed correctly. What are the topics?

Can you work out the six topics?

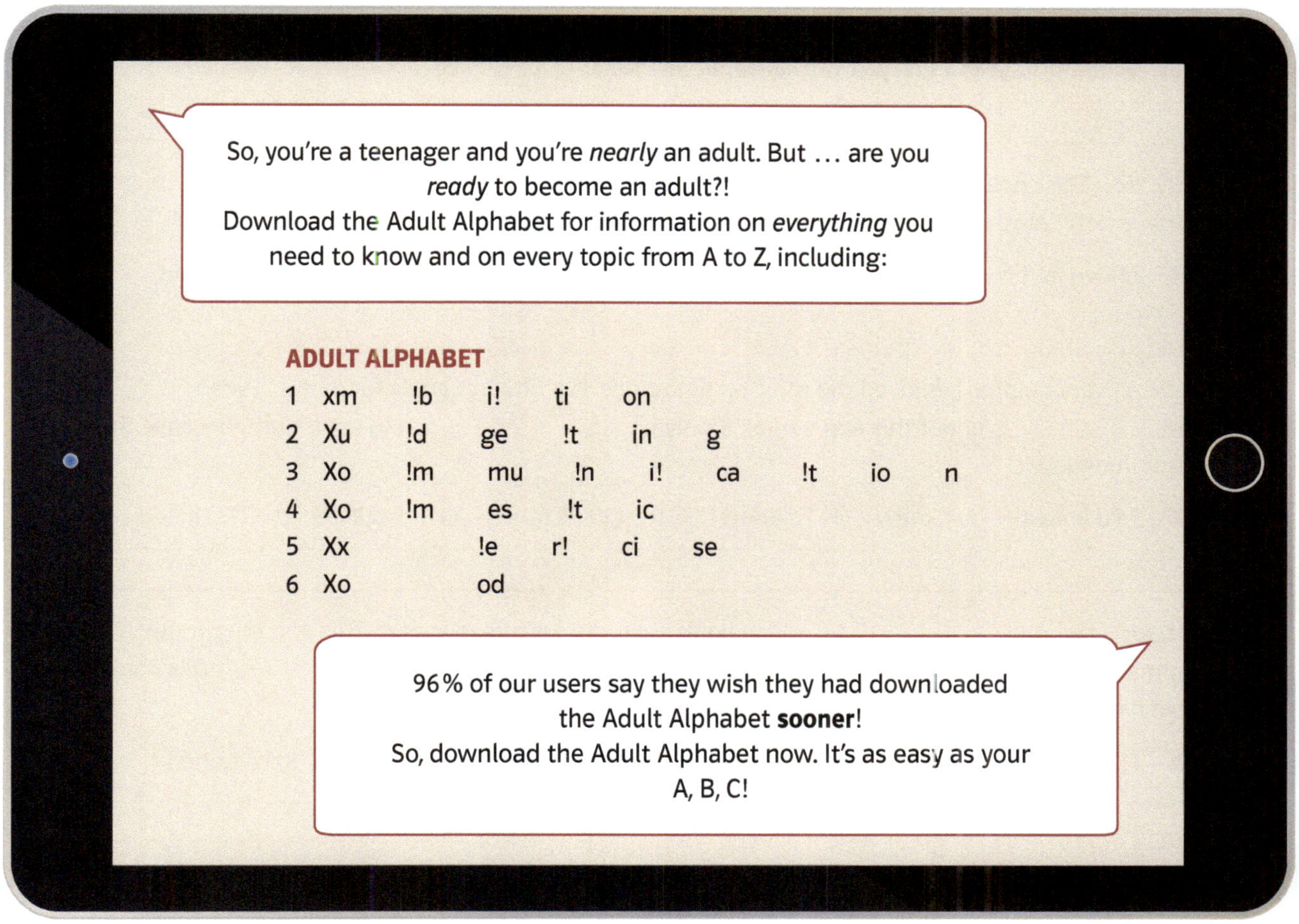

1 ………………………… 2 ………………………… 3 …………………………

4 ………………………… 5 ………………………… 6 …………………………

What is the missing code? Write the numbers and unlock the padlock!

- the number of the topic that is about social skills
- the number of the topic that is about preparing meals
- the number of the topic that is about money

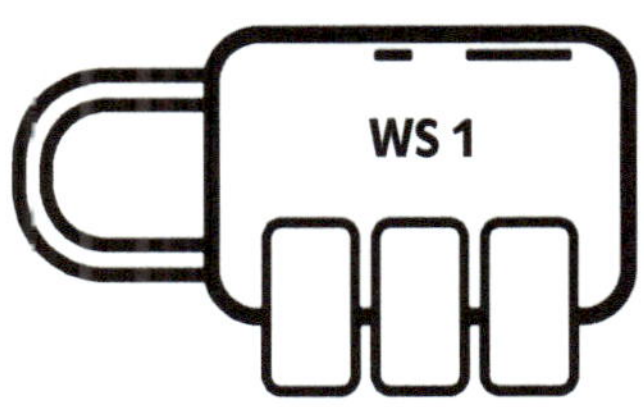

Edu Breakout Englisch – Escape Games für die 9./10. Klasse
ISBN 978-3-12-506685-4

Clues used ✓		
①	②	③

Can you complete the reviews?

Situation

Well done! You worked out the topics!

You think the app sounds great, so you start to download it. However, there is a **subscription fee**, and it is very expensive. You decide to stop the download, but another message pops up.

subscription fee *Abonnenementgebühr*

Can you complete the reviews?

IS THE SUBSCRIPTION FEE TOO EXPENSIVE?
Don't worry – if you can complete these reviews from our satisfied customers, then your subscription is FREE for the first year. Plus, you can cancel at any time!

Tammy, 15: This could be a great app. If only this app [A] .... so many technical problems. The words don't always display correctly and it's annoying. I wish they [B] .... fix it!

A (1) weren't having (2) didn't have (3) had **B** (4) will (5) can (6) would

Leon, 16: Very helpful. I enjoyed the topic on ambitions. I've now set goals for myself. I wish [C] .... about this app earlier. If only I [D] .... to my friends, because they all recommended it!

C 7 I'd known (8) I knew (9) I'd know **D** (10) listened (11) had listened (12) listen

Carlos, 16: I wish [E] .... my bank accounts organised sooner. This app taught me about managing money and I've now got two savings accounts. If only [F] .... this earlier, I would have more savings now!

E (13) I to get (14) I had got (15) I got **F** (16) I did (17) I've done (18) I'd done

Sofia, 15: I used this app to prepare for an interview for a part-time job. I got it! (I wish the pay [G] .... !) I had applied for other jobs in the past, but I didn't get any. Who knows? If [H] .... got this app earlier, I might have got one of those other jobs!

G (19) were higher (20) will be higher (21) is higher
H (22) only I (23) only I'd (24) only I've

What is the missing code? Add the numbers of the correct answers together and unlock the padlock!

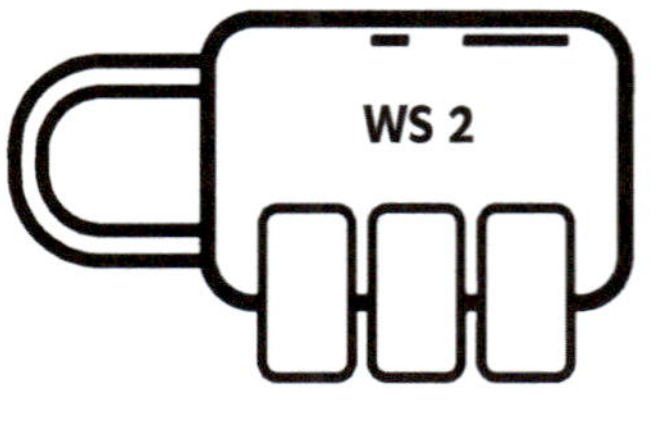

Edu Breakout Englisch – Escape Games für die 9./10. Klasse
ISBN 978-3-12-506685-4
Alles Digitale auf allango.net

Can you complete the message?

Clues used ✓		
①	②	③

Situation

Well done! You completed the reviews!

You have now downloaded the app and you have **registered your details.** It's a great app and you're going to review it in your blog. Then a new window pops up.

to register one's details *persönliche Daten eingeben*

Can you complete the message? Add only, wish and a verb from the list below in the correct form:

be enjoy know say see share

ENTER OUR MONTHLY PRIZE DRAW TO WIN A LAPTOP!
What do you have to do? Imagine you are already an adult.
Write a message to your past teenage self! Here's an example to practise on.

Dear Past Me,

How are you? If [1] .... I could [2] .... some wisdom with you (or me?) as the journey to adulthood begins.

Firstly, don't worry about trying new things or not succeeding. If [3] .... you were able to [4] .... that 'mistakes' aren't the end of the world – they are an opportunity to learn and grow.

I [5] .... I [6] .... that your interests matter. They will bring friendships and happiness to you when things are tough. If [7] .... you would [8] .... brave and follow your dreams!

What else do I [9] .... I could [10] .... to Past Me? I [11] ....
I [12] .... my free time more, because there is less free time when you become an adult.

Well, good luck Past Me! See you in the future!

Love,

Future Me

What is the missing code? Write the numbers and unlock the padlock!

- the number of past perfect answers
- the total number of wish answers
- the total number of *only* answers

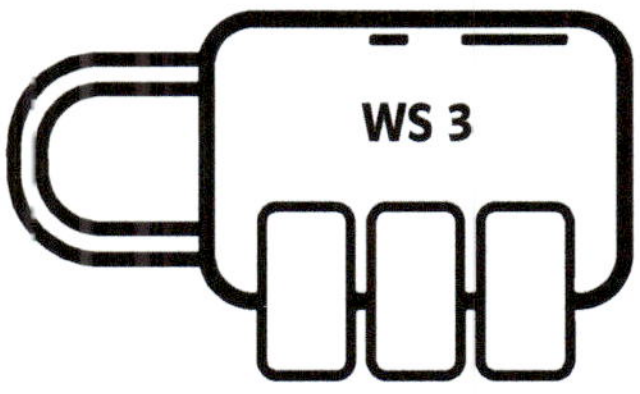

Alles Digitale auf allango.net

Edu Breakout Englisch – Escape Games für die 9./10. Klasse
ISBN 978-3-12-506685-4

Transcript – Audio of Escape game 18 – Gaming

A By 2030, do you think artificial intelligence will have transformed the gaming industry?

[pause]

B Do you think augmented reality games will shape the future of outdoor entertainment?

[pause]

C Within the next few years, do you think virtual reality headsets will have lost their popularity?

[pause]

D Do you think holographic gaming will replace traditional console gaming by 2040?

[pause]

E By next summer, do you think virtual reality games will have entered the mainstream entertainment?